DAVID GOMES
When Faith Triumphs

Anne Washburn McWilliams

214

BROADMAN PRESS
Nashville, Tennessee

Unless otherwise noted, Scripture quotations are from the King James Version of the Bible.

Scripture quotations marked (RSV) are from the Revised Standard Version of the Bible, copyrighted 1946, 1952, © 1971, 1973.

Scripture quotations marked (TLB) are from *The Living Bible*. Copyright © Tyndale House Publishers, Wheaton, Illinois, 1971. Used by permission.

© Copyright 1981 • Broadman Press

All rights reserved.

4272-26

ISBN: 0-8054-7226-6

Dewey Decimal Classification: B

Subject heading: GOMES, DAVID // BAPTISTS—BRAZIL

Library of Congress Catalog Card Number: 81-66292

Printed in the United States of America

To my dear friend
Rosalee Mills Appleby
Missionary emeritus, Brazil

Faith is a seed. . . . The seed has the tree in itself. . . . Then the tree brings forth seeds multiplied. . . . Thus, the fruit of a Christian is other Christians. Some trees are more fruitful than others, according to the amount of sun and breeze each gets. So closeness to Jesus, the Sun of righteousness, can improve the yield of the Christian's branches.

David Gomes

Foreword

For twenty-five years I have known and appreciated the ministry of David Gomes. He has been a faithful friend for these many years. He is pastor of one of the outstanding churches in Rio de Janeiro and was a vitally important part of our city-wide crusade in the great Maracana Stadium there some years ago. At the same time he was serving as president of the Brazilian Bible Society and a great Baptist leader. He is an honored alumnus of Southwestern Baptist Theological Seminary in Fort Worth. He is recognized as one of the foremost religious leaders throughout South America.

For years he has been a devoted husband and a loving father as well as being one of the greatest soul-winners and most dedicated ministers that I have ever known. His life story is one that has thrilled, challenged, stirred, and inspired all who have known him over the years and his ministry has blessed literally millions of people!

My team and I have worked with him directly and indirectly for these many years, and we have often remarked that he is one of the most radiant Christian servants and spiritually dynamic leaders in twentieth-century Christendom. I highly esteem his friendship and commend his God-anointed ministry in Brazil and throughout the entire world.

BILLY GRAHAM

Montreat, North Carolina

Preface

This book had its beginnings in 1969 when David Gomes walked into my office with the *Baptist Record* editor, Joe T. Odle. Gomes entered in a blaze of glowing enthusiasm, quoting Mark 11:22, and saying, "Nothing is impossible to God."

For ten years, off and on, I have been collecting information about him, from numerous missionaries and other individuals, from his own journals and letters. Gomes translated these from the Portuguese onto tape for me. Mrs. Boots Thompson of Morehead City, North Carolina, transcribed the tapes. Mrs. Myra Morgan of Florence, Mississippi, typed the final draft.

Gomes has visited my husband, W. D., and me at our house in Clinton, Mississippi, and I have been to Brazil to meet his family and see some of the places where he has lived.

In this book, I have tried especially hard to be honest and objective. I hope the reader will see David as he actually is—dedicated, but certainly not a saint without faults, sorrows, problems, and struggles.

I sincerely pray that those who read this story will find an example of encouragement and inspiration. Pastors and lay people, indeed, every Christian who note Gomes's creative evangelism techniques will see that to be successful they must be accompanied by an unswerving faith and a constant fellowship with God through prayer.

Woman's Missionary Union members and other Southern Baptists will get a glimpse of the distance their mission prayers and dollars have traveled in Brazil. In this one life alone, how far the ripples from small stones cast have spread! I hope they will be inspired to give and pray even more boldly in the future for missions in Brazil and around the world, and that they will be filled with the desire to proclaim the message in their own spheres of living with the same faith and missionary zeal they have seen in the life of David Gomes.

Contents

Introduction

The one hundredth anniversary of Southern Baptist mission work in Brazil will be celebrated in 1982. For at least sixty-six of those one hundred years, missionaries have had a direct influence on the lives of David Gomes and his family—since the time when his mother was baptized by a Southern Baptist missionary in 1916. As I thought of Southern Baptists' Bold Mission Thrust to proclaim the gospel to every person in the world by the year 2000, I realized that David Gomes, a Brazilian Baptist, is a man who has the deep commitment needed by every Christian if we are to reach that goal.

He is one among many colleagues in Brazil who have influenced Baptist work in their own country and throughout the world. As William L. C. Richardson pointed out in *Brazilian Obsession,* in less than one hundred years of existence, Brazilian Baptists have become one of the major bodies in the Baptist World Alliance. Their evangelistic and missionary spirit has made them such a dynamic body.

Southern Baptist missionaries arrived in Brazil in 1881, and the first Portuguese-language Baptist church in Brazil was formed in Salvador on October 15, 1882. In 1980 Southern Baptists had 301 missionaries in the country's 22 states, four territories, and federal district.

In turn, Brazilians have organized their own home and foreign mission boards and appointed missionaries themselves. The Brazilian Baptist Convention, with 5,000 baptized believers, was organized in 1907. In early 1981 they had 550,000 members in over 3,000 churches. At least 80 new churches were organized in 1980. A goal of 700,000 Baptists in Brazil has been set for reaching by 1982, the centennial year. They had in January, 1981, 316 home missionaries and 63 foreign missionaries, the latter serving in Argentina, Paraguay, Uruguay, Venezuela, Bolivia, Portugal, Spain, France, Mozambique, South Africa, USA, and Canada.

Yet, from among the many, I chose David Gomes because he is the most enthusiastic Christian witness that I have ever known. I believe there are lessons in his life many Christian witnesses might like to learn.

Others have agreed with me. Delphino Eugenio Vieira, a Brazilian Baptist pastor, said, "For me, David Gomes is a living testimony of what God can do through a man who submits himself without reservation to God."

Bill Agee, a Texas pastor, returned from Rio with the conclusion, "David Gomes is a man who beholds the glory of each day, each person, each opportunity and has found the joy of the abundant life as few others have discovered it."

"His heart is literally on fire to win others for Christ," wrote Theodore Adams, former president of the Baptist World Alliance.

"All he wants is to make God known to people," said Gomes's wife, Haydee.

Few in this century, I would venture to guess, have had as profound an influence for Christ on as many persons as has David Gomes. What are the secrets of his effectiveness as an evangelist? Why is he such a joyous witness? Answers to these are more fully revealed in this book, but I list brief reasons here:

His extraordinary faith. He believes that if God gave us the Great Commission he will help us to obey it. Gomes is sure that bold evangelism efforts will work because God promised that through him all things are possible to the believer. Gomes doesn't talk just about what can be done; he gets out and starts doing things. "Of course," he wrote, "you have noticed that Jesus never said, 'My faith hath healed thee,' or 'My faith hath saved thee,' but 'your faith.' I feel that when we believe, really and truly believe, things happen."

His thorough knowledge of the Bible. He places full emphasis on the Bible in the communication of his faith. "David Gomes is our Herschel Hobbs," stated J. Reis Pereira, editor of *O Jornal Batista.* "He has been responsible for our Bible Questions and Answers column for more than twenty years and in so doing he is the best teacher of our Baptist people in Brazil."

His belief in and constant practice of prayer. No decision, no action is taken without his first talking it over with God. He has complete faith in the promises of God to hear and answer prayer. To Gomes, prayer is praising, as well as asking.

The use of innovative ideas in evangelism. Bill Agee reported after a visit to David's church, "I was impressed with his innovative ideas. David is a creative thinker for God and is willing to experiment with new techniques of trying to reach people for Christ. This is a bit unusual for a man of his age." Some of these ideas and techniques are presented in chapters 20—23.

Concerning this individuality, Fred Hawkins, missionary member of the Church of Hope, told Haydee, "God made David and threw away the recipe."

His dependence on the Holy Spirit. David said, "The desire to apply evangelism grows, but I do not force anything. It just comes naturally. This thing of innovative methods is so much of the Holy Spirit that I really deserve no credit at all. The idea for the thirteen-hour prayer service we had on the church's thirteenth anniversary came from above, and the results were amazing. I try to depend on the Holy Spirit completely."

His way with words. He presents the gospel with clarity and power. With an inborn sense of the dramatic, David uses picturesque language, many figures of speech both in writing and in preaching.

A radiant optimism, a contagious enthusiasm. He thinks big. He believes that Christians can't be shortsighted but must attempt big things if they are going to win the world for Christ. Though something may look impossible to us, it does not look that way to God, for he can see the future.

His genuine love for people of all classes and his ability to identify with and show that he deeply cares for each individual. Of course, friendliness and enthusiasm are natural Brazilian traits. Aaron Cohen in *Rio de Janeiro,* said that "a *carioca* will call you by your first name the first time you meet, and by the second time he will be your childhood friend, patting you on the back affectionately

and hugging you in the middle of the street, celebrating that wonderful event of two people meeting."

Beyond this natural friendliness, though, David's caring is of a
deeper caliber, and he is able to make the person with him know
that he cares. This, I think, is a chief reason so many respond to his
witnessing. As David talks with an individual, that person feels the
love that is transmitted, the importance he is given as an individual,
and thus can believe Jesus loves him in the same way.

Even though thousands of letters have come to David from listeners to his radio program, the Bible School of the Air, every
report of a new believer still sets off in him a burst of ecstatic joy.

One morning, when I was in Rio at the home of Dorine Hawkins Stewart, David came rushing in, letters in hand: "Listen! This
man says he is the one lost sheep! He wrote 'Last night I heard you
say on the radio that the ninety and the nine are saved, and one
sheep is lost. I am that lost sheep. I want to know how I can be
saved.' Can you imagine that? How wonderful are the ways of
God!"

Another letter was from Guilhermo Coelho of Itauna, who had
heard David's message at 3:30 in the morning and had accepted
Jesus. He wanted a Bible.

"This Coelho is from the town where I was born. I am going to
take him a Bible myself!"

Several days later David and I were in Itauna, with his sister,
Francisca, and his nephew, Aurelio. Though David had been in
meetings in Sao Paulo and Campinas for two days and had ridden
two consecutive nights on buses (one night on a "bed-bus"), he was
still full of energy and determined to deliver the Bible.

Coelho's address turned out to be a sort of suburb of Itauna,
several miles out into the country. The little village had dirt trails for
streets, dozens of children, dogs, pony carts, and chickens.

Inquiries about Coelho's house got mixed responses from people by the roadside. Finally we saw a lone man sitting in the doorway of an empty building. David asked, "Do you know Guilhermo
Coelho?"

"I am he."

The dark-haired, thin man was astonished that David would come to see him and kept apologizing because he had not shaved that day and was wearing his house slippers. He had been ill and for that reason had been out of work for several weeks. During the late nights when he could not sleep he had listened to the radio. Overjoyed to have a Bible, he asked all of us to return with him to his house. His wife was not home, but evidently several families shared the house. Two old women were in the living room, as well as a young woman with a baby. On the wall, over a door, hung a crucifix.

We sat down and David talked to each woman about her relationship to Jesus. All of us joined hands in a circle as he prayed and led in the singing of a hymn and then in the Lord's Prayer.

That night I went with David to a family reunion at his brother Isaac's house in Belo Horizonte. After a feast celebrating David's thirty-fourth year in the ministry and lots of family fellowship, David was still leading in choruses and telling stories of God's goodness at ten o'clock.

His willingness to use all his gifts, all his time, all his money for God's purposes.

His practice of life-style evangelism. I got a glimpse of this too. David and Haydee and I drove to Petropolis, a resort city in the mountains north of Rio. During a terrific rainstorm, we stopped to eat lunch in an outdoor cafe beside the river that divides the town. An awning sheltered us from the rain and most of the wind, but I was still so cold I was shivering. I decided to go to the car to get my coat; Haydee went with me to unlock the door while I held the umbrella.

Two lovely young girls were sitting at the table next to ours, each with a glass of beer. While Haydee and I were gone, David opened a conversation with the girl nearest him.

"How does that beer taste? Is it good?"

"You never drank any?"

"No, I am a missionary." David believes that all Christians are missionaries.

At that moment one of the girls spied a "Bible School of the

Air" pin on his lapel and asked what it stood for. He told her that he answers questions about the Bible on radio. By this time, Haydee and I had returned to the table.

Her curiosity aroused, she began asking questions. Haydee joined in and began to answer some of them too. All three were speaking Portuguese. But I knew, without asking, the conversational topic, for I had a feeling that the Holy Spirit was present with us in that small restaurant.

After we finished our lunch, Haydee and I said good-bye to the girls and returned to the van, but David remained. In a few moments, he joined us. He was so happy he could not stop repeating, "She accepted Jesus! The girl accepted Jesus! I asked her if she would accept him, and she said yes she wanted to, but she didn't know how. I took her hand and prayed with her. She was trembling. She asked God to forgive her sins, and she surrendered her heart to Jesus! I gave her the name of the Baptist pastor here, and she said she will go to see him.

"Oh, God meant that we should stop here, and that you should go to the car to get your coat, so I could have a moment to speak to her. Otherwise, I might not have opened the conversation."

We drove directly from Petropolis to the airport in Rio, but my 2:45 flight for Porto Alegre had been cancelled. David made reservations for me on a plane leaving at 6 PM and suggested that in the meantime he and I ride a city bus around Governor's Island. During brief lulls in our conversation on the bus, he spoke to the man behind us, the young woman in front of us, and the man across the aisle. I did not understand the conversation, but I noticed that he gave them Scripture portions and literature concerning his radio Bible program.

(Much later he wrote me about the answer to a prayer he prayed that afternoon. At the Church of Hope the night before, fifteen persons had made professions of faith and been instructed to meet at the church early Monday evening. Since David, the pastor of the church, stayed with me until time for my plane to leave, he missed the meeting. His associate pastor, Geremias Bento da Silva, his son-in-law, had to attend a seminary class and could not go to the church. When David realized he would be too late to make it to the church, he prayed "Lord, send someone to meet with those people." A lovely woman, a faithful member of the church, suddenly had an urgent feeling that she must go immediately to the church. When she arrived, she saw she was the only one present to instruct the new converts who were already there waiting. And she did.)

Today David is not as much in the center of Baptist affairs as when he was executive secretary of the Home Mission Board of the Brazilian Baptist Convention (Home Mission Board). But during the decade of the '70s, he served as vice-president of the national Radio and Television Board, chairman of the Education Committee for the national convention, and chairman of the Spiritual Mobilization Committee for the 1974 Billy Graham Crusade in Rio. David also served as first vice-president and president of his state Baptist convention, first vice-president of the Brazilian Baptist Convention, and as a member of the committee under leadership of Rubens Lopes planning for the Second National Campaign of Evangelism in 1980.

Many of those he had influenced have in turn had a part in winning hundreds of others to Christ. For example: *Nilson Fanini,* pastor of one of the largest Baptist churches in Brazil, the First Baptist Church of Niteroi. He has served as president of the national Baptist convention and vice-president of the Baptist World Alliance and preaches on a television program, *Reencounter,* which shows all over the country with an estimated 40 million viewers. Fanini has been called the Billy Graham of Brazil. During one four-day crusade in Recife in 1979, in which he preached, 600 professions of faith were recorded.

Fanini was won to Christ through David's preaching in Curitiba in 1944. Then when David started teaching nights at the South Brazil Seminary, one of his first students in theology was Fanini.

David also influenced *Samuel Mitt,* serving in Bolivia, now president of the Baptist seminary in Curitiba, Parana. Formerly he was a home missionary and for ten years was executive secretary of the Home Mission Board.

When Mitt was pastor of the Floresta Church in Porto Alegre,

David visited the city to speak on home missions. After the meeting, the pastor and David ate lunch at a deacon's house. During the conversation, Mitt spoke out, "When some young people come forward for missions, Brother Gomes is very happy, but when the pastor of a church surrenders himself, he does not say much."

That morning Samuel had stepped down to surrender his life for missions but David had thought he had come to pray the closing prayer!

During Mitt's 10 years with the Home Mission Board, 36 new churches were organized, 72 new cities and towns were entered, 5,268 new converts were baptized, and 170 new missionaries were appointed.

Waldomiro Tymshak, executive secretary of the Brazilian Foreign Mission Board (1980) entered the ministry as the result of the preaching of David Gomes.

Edna Pinto de Morais was for ten years the national leader of GAs of Brazilian Baptist WMU (1964-1974). Born in Maceio, she heard a sermon by David on the last night of a Congress in Recife in 1955. The message convinced her she was ready to leave everything and to do the will of God.

Albertina Ramos da Silva was a student in Tocantinia at a Baptist high school directed by Home Mission Board missionaries when she heard a sermon preached by David. He based the message on a passage from Luke emphasizing Jesus as the best friend. The timid girl gave her heart to Jesus and took him as her best friend.

Later she entered the Seminary of Christian Educators in Recife. It took her seven years to get her degree because, with few funds, she had to work in many jobs to earn money for school. But with her jobs and several scholarships and the encouragement of the director, Martha Hairston, Albertina was graduated from the seminary and was appointed as a missionary to Mozambique. She was teaching in the Baptist institute in Lourenco Marques and helped prepare for the evangelistic campaign David held in that African city in 1974. (Later, because of political unrest in Mozambique, she was reassigned to the Azores.)

Selma, daughter of *Angelina Pereira Leitao,* a home missionary in Goias, surrendered her life to become a home missionary also. While she was living in Tocantinopolis, she heard an appeal by David for young people to give their lives to missions. She wanted to begin mission work right away. He told her, "The daughter of the missionary must know more than the missionary" and encouraged her to go on to college and seminary. She enrolled at the seminary in Recife where her mother had studied.

As a student Selma said, "At times when I am confronted with difficult problems, I remember some of the marvelous experiences Pastor David has told of God proving his faith and I become reanimated, knowing that his God is the same as my God who has been marvelous to me."

Part I
The Seed: 1919-1949

David Gomes

I saw him just a boy,
Earnest and vibrant,
Aggressive and independent of spirit,
Gazing out upon a world
He had resolved to conquer.

I saw him again
As an idealistic youth,
Alive with Christian faith,
Uneasy with an inward urge,
With ears attent to the Christian call
To which he never turned his back,
Nor dodged its bristles.

I saw him
After the years had gone by.
The storms had taken their toll
And left a path of broken boughs
Where once the bushes grew,
And promised the lush woodland.

I saw him yesterday,
Tall and strong,
Aged and straight,
Still intact—determined.
He had not conquered all the world,
But as he looked down from the heights,
He saw the lower pinnacles
Where he had passed and camped.
There he had left the multitudes,
Gathered in his wake.

HAFFORD BERRY,
Missionary Emeritus, Brazil

1

Before Being Born – Chosen

Before I formed thee . . . I knew thee; . . . and I ordained thee a prophet unto the nations (Jer. 1:5).

Jose could not resist a peek at the baby in the hammock, but quickly he turned away. "Sometimes I think God doesn't know what he is doing!" he burst out.

He picked up a ball that lay neglected on the floor. "God took Levi away," he cried, "and he took Isa away, and now he gives me this tiny one." The tears filled his hazel eyes and rolled down his suntanned cheeks. They trickled into the corners of his thick black moustache.

"I loved Levi. He was so smart and so sweet. But I don't know what this David will be like."

Franquelina, from across the room, assured her husband that God always knows what he is doing.

Two days before Christmas, 1919, David Gomes had entered the world in Itauna, Brazil, in the state of Minas Gerais.

The Three Brothers, tallest of the mountains that surrounded Itauna, stood like green-clad guards, offering protection to the houses that sprawled along the banks of the twisting, red-brown river and decorated the foothills with pastel colors.

In a cramped house on Matriz Street, the Christmas spirit had not arrived for the Gomes family. Sorrow hung heavy as iron on the hearts of its inhabitants. Summer heat rays of high noon danced on the dull orange roof tiles. In a corner of the kitchen, water boiled in a kettle on the built-in stove of adobe brick.

For Franquelina Gomes, this new baby would be her eleventh. Of the other ten, the first two had died as infants. Six weeks before David's birth, two-year-old Levi died, falling from a table. Sorrow, though, had not finished with the house on Matriz Street. Bright-eyed Isa had lived six years before she had died of diphtheria early that December.

Conceicao, oldest of her daughters, added charcoal to the fire in the stove. *It doesn't seem like Christmas without Isa,* Conceicao thought. She brushed away a tear. Through the window she could see her father in the narrow courtyard by the japoticaba tree. When the midwife came out of the bedroom, nodding and smiling, Conceicao ran to the door and called, "Papa, Papa! Christmas has come! We have another boy!"

Franquelina was as grieved as Jose at the loss of the children, but she felt assured of God's comforting presence. She did not doubt that the baby was an answer to her prayer for another son or that God's long-range plan included something special for the child.

As she held her baby close, she thought that the David in the Bible must have had dark hair and eyes like this one.

Much childbearing had not ruined Franquelina's loveliness. She was tall, her high cheek bones and a long slender neck giving her an aristocratic look. Her wide mobile mouth, if not engaged in animated conversation, was curved in a smile. She was a vivacious extrovert.

Her large, brown eyes softened as she remembered the early years of her marriage and thought of the circumstances that led to the dedication of her youngest child to God.

Ever since Franquelina da Conceicao had married Jose Gomes, he had been working for the railroad. The mines of Minas Gerais kept needing more railroads to transport their products to the seaports. The state was full of gold, iron, diamonds, manganese, amethysts, and aquamarines. Trains lugged their heavy loads through the lush mountains to the Atlantic. They skirted granite cliffs, chugged through villages, and went slinking through the jungle.

From one town in Minas to another, the railroad had transferred Jose. In Pitangui, he had gotten a promotion in 1913 and became the *guarda-chaves* (keeper of the keys), or switchman. It was a good position, but gradually the work hours stretched longer and longer.

As Adolph, his co-worker, stayed drunk most of the time, Jose was forced to learn the Morse code himself. Adolph's wife, Isa, poured her troubles into the ears of large-hearted Franquelina, who kept saying, "If only we had a Catholic church in Pitangui, maybe we could get the priest to pray for Adolph."

Though Franquelina was much interested in religion, she could never quite grasp the peace and hope she sought. They were always flitting away, like fireflies in the dark. Always she had been faithful in church activities. By keeping all the rules of the church, she felt that she might eventually find happiness. Her good deeds and loyal service had won for her many medals from her church. Yet, deep within, admitted only to herself, she knew she had not found satisfaction in candles and clay images.

"How could we pay a priest to come to Pitangui?' Isa asked.

"I can wash clothes for a few families." This she did and with Isa's help began to pay a priest to visit the town regularly.

The next year the railroad transferred Jose to Juatuba. At the public fountain one day his wife waited to fill her water pots. Two women in line seemed friendly, so she mentioned to them the need for a Catholic church.

"But the Bible forbids bowing to images," one of them told her. In anger Franquelina walked away, her water pots unfilled.

Back home, Francisca (David's sister) looked up from her task of making coconut oil soap to tell the good news! "A letter from Isa! She and Adolph are moving here!"

When Franquelina met the couple at the train station, she was bursting with the news, "Two families live here who say they don't believe in praying to the saints."

Isa's surprising reply was like a dipperful of cold water in her face: "Maybe they have a Bible I can borrow. If they are Baptists, I hope they plan to start a church."

Since Isa had last seen her friend, she had heard a sermon by a Baptist minister. Two ideas had stuck with her: Any person can pray directly to God without going through a human mediator. Salvation is by faith, not works. The minister had read from a Bible and ever since Isa had been anxious to read the Bible for herself.

"If you plan to be their friend, then I can't be your friend. I can't even invite you to dinner today." With that, Franquelina flounced home.

Nevertheless, Isa did get a Bible. She went to see Franquelina and read it aloud. Franquelina started sewing on her machine to drown out the words. Never before had she heard the Bible read, or read it herself. It had always been forbidden. When Isa had finished reading, she sang "Standing on the Promises." Though Franquelina would not say so, she liked the hymn.

Isa found out that Baptist worship services were being held nearby and began to attend. She asked Franquelina to go, but she would not.

A few weeks later, Isa begged, "Please come with me this time. I have decided to commit my life to Christ, and I am to be baptized in the river."

"No!"

"Then I will go," Jose interrupted.

His wife laughed loudly. "I don't need to go to the river. I can take my bath at home."

The day of her baptism Isa left a message for her friend: "As the Holy Spirit has cleansed my heart, he will cleanse your heart. I know that before long you will accept Christ too."

Francisca and Conceicao went with Jose to the baptismal service. They returned home eager to tell about the day.

"A missionary was there, Mama," reported Conceicao. Her black eyes sparkled. "His name is Daniel Crosland."

"He had a suitcase full of Bibles," Francisca interrupted in her bubbly, enthusiastic way, her dark curls bouncing.

"Stop!" Franquelina commanded. "What you saw there, forget! I am tired of hearing about the Baptists." But she was to hear more.

Soon Jose transferred to Itauna. He and his family moved across the railroad track from the grimy train station. Every day they listened to the trains come and go with their loads from the iron mines.

Early one morning Franquelina heard someone clapping outside the door. "*Bom dia!* What do you want?"

"Would you please let me have a can of water?"

She politely gave the woman a can of water every day for

several days until her new neighbor asked, "Would you come to visit our Baptist church?"

"Leave my house, please, and don't come back. I will not give you water again."

"*Obrigada,*" the woman said. "*Ate logo.*" ("Thank you. Farewell, for a little while.")

One afternoon Jose told her that Florentino Ferreira, a former railroad worker, had moved to Itauna as pastor of the Baptist church. "He's coming to visit us."

Before Franquelina could voice the protest on her lips, Jose stopped her: "Be nice to him. He's my friend."

That night Ferreira made the first of many visits to the Gomes home. He asked the family to church, but Franquelina always refused. Finally one January day he told her, "I have to go back to the seminary soon. Before I leave, I want you to hear me preach, just once."

At last she gave in. When she arrived on Sunday morning, the congregation was singing "Standing on the Promises." Since most had their own hymnals, Conceicao begged her mother to buy one.

"No. We can't pay for it."

Conceicao began to cry. The preacher, to restore order, said, "I will sell a songbook to you, and you can pay later."

Someone in the congregation spoke up and told the pastor he should not sell a hymnal on Sunday. Franquelina got mad and took her children home.

However, Florentino did not give up. He returned to the Gomes home that afternoon and said, "Tonight is the last sermon I will preach here as pastor. Please come back."

That February evening in 1915 Florentino chose as his text, "Today is the day of salvation." At the invitation, the woman who had told her husband that morning, "I shall never change," decided to follow Jesus. That night the Holy Spirit convicted her of her sins. The Savior, the Christ of the cross, the Christ of the resurrection, became real to her at last. The peace she had tried to find by doing good works and keeping all the outward rules of the Church at last was hers.

On May 16, 1915, Franquelina was baptized by Daniel Crosland, the same missionary who had baptized Isa, in the Saint John River where it widened into a pool below the railroad bridge in Itauna.

Crosland was one of the earliest Baptist missionaries to witness for Christ in Minas. He was a contemporary of Solomon Ginsburg. Only thirty-five years earlier, in 1881, William and Anne Bagby had landed in Brazil and thirty-four years earlier, in 1882, the first Brazilian Baptist church had been organized.

When the railroad sent Jose to work in a town with no school, he was displeased. His employer refused to send him to another place. Consequently, Jose lost his temper, and the agent fired him. Nothing was left but to move back to Pitangui where Franquelina's parents lived.

By this time, Jose and Conceicao had also accepted Christ and been baptized. People in Pitangui heard that the Gomes family had become Protestants. Others in Minas, as fanatical as Franquelina had been, began to treat the Gomeses with contempt.

A priest (Pitangui at last had a resident one) ordered that nobody walk on the sidewalk in front of the Gomes home. Nobody was to send the family food or clothing. No one was to give Jose a job. When Franquelina's mother dared to defy the order and take food to her daughter and grandchildren, she would not enter but tossed the packages through a window.

In this time of trial, Franquelina kept singing "Standing on the Promises." She tried to wash clothes to make a little money, but women would throw debris into the stream above her washing place on the river bank or wade into the water to muddy it. She planted a garden and occasionally sold a few bundles of wood.

Without a job, without money, Jose in desperation decided to visit one of his brothers to ask for a loan.

Only a little rice remained in the house. Franquelina cooked it with some vegetables and said to her husband, "You take this, for you must travel a long way. The Lord will provide food for us tomorrow."

After Jose had gone, she fed the children the few leftovers. Later that night she sat alone, mending clothes while the children slept. She had not eaten and did not know where the next meal would come from.

Suddenly she heard a voice: "Fear not, daughter. Believe in the Father." She walked to the kitchen, but no one was there. Back in her room she began praying. Again she heard the words, "Daughter, fear not; believe in the Father." That night marked the end of the difficult time and the beginning of better days.

The next morning, when the older daughters were leaving for school, their mother told them, "You must go to school without bread or coffee today, but please don't tell anyone you haven't eaten. Don't allow people to pity you."

When the teacher called the roll, she learned that two students from a wealthy family were absent; she asked the Gomes girls to go find out why. At the home they were fed because it was the custom always to serve guests. Spread before them was a feast: coffee, milk, cheese, crackers, butter, and three kinds of bread.

That same morning the railroad agent sent Franquelina a message saying that he had made a discovery. Jose had formerly made an overpayment of dues; now the railroad wanted to rectify the mistake and return his money. The excited woman sent word to her husband, who immediately returned home. Usually, when Jose stopped at the butcher shop, he held up his hat and said, "As this hat is here, I'll pay you the first day I get some money." But this day, the moment he arrived, he paid the bill.

On the way home he heard someone calling from the roadside, "Gomes! Gomes! I need a fence built. Do you want the job?"

Soon the family moved back to Itauna to Matriz Street, and Jose was given back his job.

One day in June, 1919, Franquelina was walking down the street when she met Florentino Ferreira, "Pastor Florentino," she said, "You remember, I asked you to pray with me that I might have another son so I could dedicate him to the Lord's work? God has answered our prayer. I am expecting my eleventh child."

As soon as Florentino heard of the child's birth, he went to see the Gomes family. While he held the baby David in his arms, he prayed with the mother, and together they dedicated him to the Lord.

2

The Seed of Faith

He that goeth forth and weepeth, bearing precious seed, shall doubtless come again with rejoicing, bringing his sheaves with him (Ps. 126:6).

Higher and higher the kite sailed, while David held the line and ran down the street as fast as his short young legs could go. Never in his life had he had enough extra money to buy the colored paper to make a proper *papagaio*. For weeks he'd begged Papa to buy him one. At last Jose had come home with a kite, the biggest his son had ever seen.

In his exhilaration, David forgot to check the kite to see if it were tied securely. Up and up into the blue sky the wonderful *papagaio* climbed. With a jerk, it separated from the line and kept on going, away and out of sight.

David started to sob, but his father told him, "Stop crying now. I have no money for another. Go wash the beans."

The boy and his brothers, Isaac and Zezé, had been assigned the job of separating the beans from the dried mud they were packed in to make them last longer. Sifting out the chaff was a tedious and boring job, so David hatched an idea.

"If we pour water over the beans the mud will melt. After that we can pour the water out and the beans will be clean." They followed his suggestions to the letter, but the beans still were definitely not clean. David paid in an unpleasant way for his bright idea.

In the Gomes family everybody had a job because money was scarce. After David, four more babies were born: Paulo, Margarida (who died as an infant), a second Isa, and Anita. (Older children still living include Conceicao, Maria Jose, Francisca, Waldemira, Zezé, and Isaac.) For the needs of so many, Jose's income was not enough.

Everyone who could add to the earning did so. The oldest daughters found jobs in the cotton mill. The younger children would climb with their mother into the edge of the mountain forest to pick up bits of firewood to sell on street corners. As the children walked in the woods, they sang hymns.

For a while, Franquelina baked cakes and candies for the boys to sell. This drew regular customers, but David and Isaac decided they could earn more by selling newspapers.

"Get up, sons!" Jose would call every morning at 5:30. Often he would advise them, "Sons, never make debts. Your father can open the door at any time, for he knows it is not a creditor calling."

When they collected their newspaper money, they would take out the tithe, as their mother had taught them to do, and save the rest for household expenses. Because David liked so well to help his mother, Zezé, and Isaac called him *Davina,* the feminine form of his name.

A merchant to whom David had sold papers handed him an extra cruzeiro as a gift. To avoid spending the money on bus fare, David walked the two miles home. His mother, thinking he had stolen the coin, commanded him to take it back; she walked with him. "This is the most honest boy I ever saw," the merchant told her. "He has never stolen anything."

Young David's favorite chore was to take his father's lunch to the railroad's ironsmith shop, where Jose fashioned bolts and clamps to fasten the rails together. The barefoot boy in short pants would squash a wide-brimmed hat over his black hair, walk down the hillside to the train tracks, and balancing himself carefully, walk along a rail, his father's lunch in a tin pail dangling from one out-stretched arm. His alert brown eyes missed little—the people he met, the chickens behind a fence, the dogs, the birds, the flowers, and the occasional snake.

He crossed the river, leaping from one railroad tie to another, not looking through the wide cracks to the brown water churning below.

His pace slowed as he started up the mountain toward the gash in the red bluff, where the iron mine began and the smithy was located. For an hour or two, he would pump the bellows to make the fire blaze higher while his father shaped the red hot iron. To his way of thinking, he was making his father's work easier.

Jose also prescribed remedies for various illnesses. People

who could not afford doctors came from small villages to ask his medical advice.

"Take this medicine and with the blessing of the Lord you will get well," Jose told each client. David memorized the remedies. In fact, most of them had been tried out on him.

Spider webs and dry coffee grounds were used to stop bleeding; vanilla bean tea was good for stomachaches; pumpkin seed for worms, tea from avocado or lime leaves for liver or kidney upsets; juice from the skin of green cotton buds for cutting fevers; herbs for headaches; and rose petals steeped in water for a laxative. A certain banana, called the silver banana, if cooked, was good for curing stomach ailments.

Patients often paid in pigs or chickens. It was a rare occasion when the Gomes family could eat a female suckling pig (leitoa).

Usually they were on a steady diet of beans and rice, so any meat was a welcomed change. David and Isaac resolved to go bird hunting to bring meat for dinner. However they only captured one big bird. When Franquelina saw it she cried, "Oh, now, we can't eat that beautiful bird. It would be too small for all of us to eat anyhow." She let it fly away.

The house on Matriz Street had little furniture, but love filled the empty spaces. Sometimes the roof leaked. No glass covered the windows, but wooden shutters opened inward to let in plenty of light and air.

Poverty during childhood proved to be an important subject for David in God's school. It prepared him for trials and losses, as well as victories. For one thing, he learned to eat anything. The bitter food, gilo, he hated. His mother would say, "You do not want gilo. Then you will eat only gilo. Son, the world is hard, and you must learn to like anything God gives you for food."

Yet life was not all work and discipline. When Jose went to Belo, he always tried to bring home two special treats—fresh water sardines and the city newspapers. Occasionally he would give the children a cruzeiro or two so they could run to Senhor Adolfo's store to buy candy wrapped in comic strips. They cut pictures from the newspapers and stored them in the big family trunk. Often

David and Isaac swam in the river. And once, for a short while, David owned a kite.

When David started to school at the Escola Estadual Augusto Goncalves, he chose the desk at front of the center row. Above the blackboard was a crucifix. Below it the teacher wrote a different motto every day, such as "The wealthy student is one who works hard and makes good grades" or "If you walk with a good person, you will become a good one too."

Tall green shutters, when opened, permitted the breezes to drift through the schoolroom. Students had planted a brazilwood tree in the rear courtyard. But David's favorite climbing tree at school was a mimosa.

As his home was a school of poverty, it was also a school of faith. His mother planted the seeds of faith which would germinate and grow and one day produce fruit. Each morning as her children left for school Franquelina would pray with each one individually. David got tired of all this praying so he tried to slip out the door unnoticed, but he got caught. His mother followed him to the door and called, "David, you have not yet prayed with me. The world is too big to enter without prayer."

Jose arrived home with dramatic news that the railroad had assigned him to be in charge of the company's warehouse in Belo Horizonte. That meant a move to a larger city, maybe a nicer house, a higher salary, and easier work for Jose.

In the spring, when the Gomes family moved to Belo, flamboyant trees dotted the city with scarlet splashes. The wide streets and tall white buildings pleased David, but the house at 423 Quiteria Street impressed him more. He felt like he had moved to the governor's palace. It had wooden floors, electricity, running water, and two sinks, one in the kitchen and one in the living room! For two months he enjoyed this splendor before his family took up residence in a smaller, less expensive house in the valley.

Belo had been built in a bowl of mountains. Downtown was at the bottom of the dish. Around it houses spread almost to the top of the mountainous rim on all sides. The warehouse where Jose worked was near the Arruba River which flowed through the downtown area parallel to the railroad. The shape of the city made it appear at evening to have numerous horizons. Hence, the city's name—Beautiful Horizon. As the sun dipped lower and lower, it looked as though there were not one, but half a dozen sunsets, red, purple, blue, gold, silver, and pink.

While David was in his fourth and last year of the primary course at the Melo Vina Grade School in Belo, a priest came every Thursday to teach the catechism.

The boy's mother instructed him, "Son, when the priest comes, please ask the teacher's permission to leave the room."

This will be fine, he thought. Perhaps many others would go out with him and they could play outdoors. However, when the priest came and David asked permission to leave, no one else asked to go with him.

At home he questioned his mother, "Could everybody else be right, and only I am wrong?"

She gave him a wise answer, "David, do you believe Jesus is the Son of God?"

"Yes, Mother."

"Then don't bother about the others. Just keep your faith."

Each Thursday the same thing would happen. Finally David asked his teacher if she thought his friends were wrong and he were the only right one. She smiled and said, "I share your beliefs. I am a Christian, and my husband is a pastor."

The Barro Preto Baptist Church was a long way across town, too far to walk. At first the streetcar driver wouldn't let anybody ride barefoot. Franquelina could not buy shoes for all her children, but poverty had not defeated her and she didn't intend that it should. She asked the Lord for a solution.

Some children she had seen playing in the streets had worn only one shoe. If she divided all the available shoes so each of her youngsters had at least one, it might work. It did. The driver could not honestly say the Gomeses were still barefoot, so he let them ride.

At ten, David was a Sunday School member but had not made a personal commitment to Christ. Like other people, he had a tendency to rebel against God. Sin and selfishness emerged in many ways. At the tailor shop where David worked afternoons after school, he lost the battle with temptation.

Jarbas, a young man who worked with him at the shop, kept sending him out to buy cigarettes and insisting he try one. When finally he did, he liked it. He began smoking a cigarette every once in a while.

His sister Waldemira's boyfriend, a Presbyterian, sometimes went with her to the Baptist Sunday School. To embarrass David, Jarbas asked Waldemira's friend, "What is the difference between a Presbyterian and a Baptist?"

Like Peter, David always spoke up first: "I think Presbyterians have an easier discipline. Their members are allowed to smoke and Baptists are not."

"Is that so?" Jarbas sneered. "Why do you smoke then?"

David dropped his head and begged, "Please, Waldy, don't tell the family I have smoked. I never will again." And he meant it.

Waldemira, as well as David's mother, had a hand in sowing the seeds of faith in David's heart. Her words and the preaching of a Southern Baptist missionary caused him to think seriously about the question of salvation.

"Being the son of Christians won't save you," he heard Waldemira tell Isaac.

The same would be true of me, he thought. *If Isaac needs forgiveness, I do too. If he is a sinner, I am one.*

Sunday morning, January 26, 1931, was hot, but David scarcely noticed. At Barro Preto Church, he sat on the fourth row listening to O. P. Maddox's sermon. He heard the first stanza of the invitation hymn, the second, the third, but would not go forward. "Jesus is calling, is tenderly calling. . . ." Another went but he held onto the pew.

Maddox, the missionary-pastor, said, "We are going to sing the last stanza. I hope another will come."

Suddenly David found himself at the front. He didn't know exactly how he had gotten there, but he told the pastor he had accepted Jesus as his Savior and wanted everyone to know it.

From that time at age eleven, David Gomes felt an assurance that his sins had been forgiven. As a missionary had baptized his mother, a missionary also baptized him. The knowledge that Jesus was with him was to sustain him through all the sadness and hard times to follow.

3

Hard Times

Thanks be to God, which giveth us the victory through our Lord Jesus Christ (1 Cor. 15:57).

In every kind of situation, people depended on Franquelina. A few months before David's baptism, she had stood the test in time of a revolution.

October 3, 1930, while David was making a delivery to Santa Teresa for the tailor, he noticed a large number of soldiers boarding all the street cars. So extraordinary did this seem to him that he rushed directly home. As he entered the door, he heard gunfire, uncomfortably close.

For several years military officers had been leading occasional protest movements against the civilian administrators of the republic. In the election of 1930, the administration-sponsored candidate had won. A revolt led by Getulio Vargas broke out.

When David first heard the shots, Jose was away at work. By this time, the family lived near the army post, dangerously near the fighting. Franquelina felt she had to get the children away to a place of safety, so she prepared to flee to Francisca's house on the other side of the city.

"It's too dangerous to try to go now," David protested.

"God will protect us. Pray for me that I will know the right route to take. While you pray, just follow me."

The wee band carefully and swiftly walked down one mountain, across the river, through the center of the city, and up the mountain on the other side. They reached Francisca's house in safety and stayed until Getulio Vargas's forces had won.

As David neared graduation from elementary school, he told his mother he wanted to be a doctor. She had never revealed to him that she had dedicated him to God before his birth and still did not.

Finding money for tuition would be a problem, but Franquelina located a school with an opening. David passed the entrance exam to the secondary school which would have two levels—*ginasio* and *colegio*. Then if he passed the test he could go directly to medical school. However, he never entered the school his mother had chosen.

When the revolution was over, the Gomes house again over-flowed with guests. Franquelina liked to have company. Anniver-saries and birthdays were celebrated with fanfare. To be hospitable and helpful came naturally to her. Though rarely sick herself, she had compassion for others who were ill. Due to the lack of hospitals in the interior, many who came to Belo to see doctors stayed with the Gomes family.

Once a young girl with a strange tropical disease arrived. Her stay lengthened. Because of the girl's unbecoming immoral be-havior, Jose asked Franquelina to send her away. Reluctantly Fran-quelina obeyed. The girl angrily packed her possessions and left.

Not long afterward, Franquelina fell ill, seriously so, for the first time in her life. Superstitious neighbors said the girl had put a hex on her. The spiritists believed that by voodoo the girl could have called misfortune on her former benefactor.

Franquelina's illness was one the doctors failed to diagnose or cure. In constant pain, she daily grew weaker and weaker.

Just at this time Jose lost his job as a result of one of his impul-sive speeches. The director of the railroad had been doing battle with a Belo Horizonte newspaper. Someone left a note for the edi-tor: "If you continue to fight me, you will be killed." The newspaper printed the note; the railroad director denied he wrote it.

On a street car, passengers read the newspaper and discussed the case. Jose, listening in, nervously rubbed his moustache and fingered his watch chain. Suddenly he grabbed a paper and roared, "That is the signature of the railroad director. He may deny it, but the handwriting is his."

Word of the occurrence traveled to the director, and he fired Jose. For the next six months, the Gomes family knew hard times—worse than any they had experienced before. Food was so scarce they even ate the peelings of sweet potatoes. But if anyone complained, Franquelina bade them to be quiet. Ill as she was, she trusted that God would provide. She never failed to tithe the little money they had.

Sweet potatoes with rice appeared on the table at least twice a day. Occasionally beans were added. Candido Goncalves, the grocer, offered credit, but Jose wanted no debts.

One afternoon David returned home to find candies spread on the table. His mother smiled and said, "Son, God has given the victory. The director has been cleared. Your father was called back to work and paid for all the time he was out." While rejoicing, David secretly thought that his father could have been able to manage his tongue better.

Steadily Franquelina's pains grew worse. A spiritist leader challenged Jose: "If you will give me permission, I will have a session here. If I don't heal your wife, you may kill my wife without fear of punishment."

The spiritist claimed he could contact departed spirits through a medium and receive useful information on health problems.

The dying Franquelina overheard the conversation and called to the spiritist, "I know in whom I believe, and I am certain he is all-powerful to keep me until that day." After the man left, she told Jose that the devil had been trying to tempt her and take her out of the hands of the Lord.

When she saw one of her daughters crying, she asked, "Have you forgotten the divine promises?" She sang one of her favorite hymns: "Trials should not frighten us nor perils and afflictions weaken our faith, for God hath promised to protect his own. Through him who loveth us we shall always be victorious."

As Franquelina talked to each of her children, she told David, "You have never given me any trouble. Continue to be a good boy, and the Lord will direct your life and you will always be a blessing." Franquelina died at age forty-nine.

By this time David was not in school at all but worked full time. In addition to his job at the tailor shop, David sold fruits at the market and worked at night, writing fillers for a newspaper, *Jornal da Manha*.

In the mornings, he cleaned the house and cooked the noonday meal. Then Isaac cooked supper. David's cooking had improved since the time he had gone to visit Francisca. She had asked him to fix rice for dinner but didn't tell him how much to cook. He opened a two-pound package, washed it, seasoned it, and fried the whole package. He added water as she had directed, but the rice swelled and swelled. It overflowed the pan so that he had to pour some into a second pan, and then into a third.

Every minute he could manage to read he did. His home library included only two volumes—the Bible and a long romance, *Guarani.* Five times he read *Guarani,* a story of Indians on the Panguenques River at Petropolis. Again and again he read the Bible.

In prayer meeting at the Barro Preto Church, David heard the tailor, his employer, talk about the high far interior of Brazil where many had never heard the gospel.

Maybe I can go and tell them, he thought. But he wanted to be a doctor. He pushed the idea of missions out of his mind.

4

Who Will Go?

Go ye . . . and lo, I am with you (Matt. 28:19-20).

"Who is willing to enter the Lord's service?" Lewis M. Bratcher asked. He described Brazil's mission needs with vividness and begged for volunteers.

Sunday morning, June 19, 1935, David had arrived early at the Barro Preto Church, in anticipation of hearing the speaker.

For nine years Bratcher, a Southern Baptist missionary, had been executive secretary of the Home Mission Board of the Brazilian Baptist Convention (Home Mission Board). Perhaps more than anyone, he had succeeded in placing missions in the hearts of Brazilian Baptists.

Ever since David had heard the tailor tell of the need for missionaries, he had not been able to forget. Now he was certain God was calling him to preach. With thirteen others, he responded to Bratcher's plea for volunteers.

Afterward he was afraid to go home and tell his father of his decision. Jose, though a Christian, had been excluded from church fellowship for a minor misdemeanor. Discipline in the Baptist church was strict.

Maybe the pastor will speak to my father, David thought. O. P. and Efigenia Maddox had been missionaries in Belo since 1918, the year before David's birth. He had often been a guest at their house. The Baptist high school, Colegio Batista, had been organized in their living room with eight students. Later Maddox had acquired the Barroso estate as the school's campus.

As usual, when David clapped at the door, Dona greeted him in her gracious, gentle way. Almost every time he came, one or two groups would be having prayer meetings in the house, but this time he didn't see anyone, except the Maddox' sons John, Samuel, and David, and their daughter, Kathleen.

"Pastor Maddox, how can I go to school? I have only one pair of trousers. I have no money. What will my father say?"

Maddox reassured him and prayed with him. Then he said, "Come, I'll go with you to talk to your father."

The young man's fears were unfounded, for Jose's attitude posed no problem.

"Go, Son!" he urged. "Go to school. I can't give you money, but I will pray for you. Pastor Maddox tells me you can work at Colegio Batista."

Miss Ray Buster, David's missionary Sunday School teacher, offered to buy his first books and pay part of his tuition. The Maddoxes arranged with Antonio Vilas Boas, a deacon in First Baptist Church, Belo Horizonte, to pay the balance of his tuition the first year.

Though his tuition was paid, he still had to work for his board. As janitor, he cleaned classrooms. As chief monitor in the boys' dorm, he was responsible for maintaining order and discipline day and night. His duties as chief monitor left little time for rest or study. In spite of his heavy load, he made excellent grades.

Seated in the classroom an hour before a French exam, he prayed intensely: "Gracious God, I could not study and you know this as well as I. Cheat I will not. You also know this. I ask your help, and I believe you will give it." He ended the prayer and reviewed the material for thirty minutes. He made a surprisingly good grade. Under the circumstances, he rated it 100.

Years later he remembered that prayer and wrote, "How often we expect a grade of 100 when we receive a grade of zero. But how often we expect zero when God gives us 100."

Once the other students buried his bedraggled shoes which he had lined with newspapers to cover the holes in the soles. "You will have to unbury them," he told the students, "because they are the only ones I have."

Usually he tried to wear a large smile so the patches on the back of his pants would not be as noticeable.

Before many months, the pastor, Munelar Mair, invited him to speak at a preaching point in Vila Bicalho. For his first sermon, he chose a text that was to become the theme of his life, "Faith in

God." From Mark 10, David told the story of blind Bartimaeus. His outline had five points: 1. What is blindness? 2. What is the difference between physical blindness and spiritual blindness? 3. Can the blind hope to see? 4. Is persistence in asking important? 5. What will be the result of faith?

He was struggling to correlate his ideas when Arnold Harrington, missionary director of the dorm, suggested, "You should say that Bartimaeus took advantage of Jesus' last trip on that road. He was blessed because he took advantage of opportunity." David remembered this observation about Bartimaeus and opportunity and put it to practice in his own life.

In his second year at Colegio Batista, tuition increased. Miss Buster told David she might find someone who could pay it if she could send his picture to her friends in the United States.

Since David didn't have a suit to wear to have his picture made, he borrowed one from J. L. Riffey, missionary director of the school. The suit was much too big, but he and Riffey stuffed it with newspapers to make it appear to fit. The photo was snapped, and Miss Buster sent it to Central Baptist Church, Clovis, New Mexico.

Soon afterward Robert Stone, owner of Stone Grain and Elevator in Clovis, began to make out checks on a regular basis for David's education. Other Sunday School class members of Central Church contributed to the fund, but David was not told the source of the money.

Four days before Lent was carnival time. Young people at Colegio Batista did not take part in the uninhibited celebrations of carnival time. One procession of samba dancers and musicians followed another in a continuous parade. Amid whirling confetti the costumed dancers swayed to the music day and night. Food and drinks were sold on the streets. Businesses closed. Servants took a leave from their jobs. Hardly anyone worked for four days.

During the fiesta time Hafford Berry, missionary teacher at the colegio, directed a Bible memorizing contest. David and Waldemira, who was also a student at the school, entered the competition. Since David never tired of reading and quoting Scripture passages, no one was surprised when he won first place.

His mother and his professors at the colegio had taught him that Scripture is truth and that when he read the Bible he was placing himself in the right environment to learn God's will.

John 15:7 made a deep impression on David: "If ye abide in me, and my words abide in you, ye shall ask what ye will, and it shall be done." He had faith that God would answer his prayers and direct his life.

In 1938, while he was on vacation in Divinópolis, the Young People's Training Union elected him president. At first, he said he didn't know how to preside. However, a friend told him he would lose a learning opportunity if he refused. He decided to try and promised himself never to turn down any responsibility offered him if he understood it to be God's orders.

The following year Frank Leavell, director of Baptist Student Union (BSU) work in the Southern Baptist Convention, arrived to initiate Baptist Student work in Brazil. He began with Colegio Batista, which then elected David the first BSU president in the country.

"Congratulations!" Leavell said and embraced David in the way he had seen Brazilians do—a bear hug, touching left cheeks and then right cheeks.

At the same time, Rosalee Appleby was elected BSU faculty advisor. She and her husband, David, had come to Belo Horizonte as missionaries in 1924. They planned to minister in the interior, but this was not to be. Only a year after the couple landed in Brazil, David Appleby died of a stomach ulcer. At home his body was laid out in the sitting room. Only a few hours later, his son David was born. The grieving mother laid the baby on his father's breast and prayed that he might be as fine a man, as dedicated to God, as his father had been. David Appleby was buried in Belo, underneath the tall palms and the blue of the tropical sky, the words of John 3:16 on his gravestone.

Dona Rosalee could not work in the interior alone, so she stayed to write curriculum materials and to help develop an orphanage. She directed the Department of History and Statistics of the Brazilian Baptist Sunday School Board.

Because few had cars, especially in the interurban areas, missionaries or church members would start Sunday Schools in homes. Students or laymen would then begin preaching services at the home mission points. Later literacy classes or medical aid services were sometimes added.

Starting such a mission in Floresta, near the Baptist school, was a project of the new BSU. David Gomes preached and directed the Sunday School. Dona Rosalee taught the Bible lesson and led the visitation. Later this Sunday School, together with a weekly preaching place in the Maddox home, constituted the Floresta Baptist Church.

To the Sunday afternoon Sunday School David wore his customary glowing smile. His enthusiasm drew the children and young people by the dozens. Soon at least one hundred were coming every Sunday. The children loved him and begged to have their new baby brothers named for him.

One afternoon David taught the congregation the hymn, "For He Is So Precious to Me." They sang it over and over.

The next day Mrs. Appleby was visiting in a newcomer's home. The woman told her, "All night long in my dreams I saw that boy standing there singing, 'So Precious Is Jesus.' I'll never forget those words." As a result, she accepted Christ as her Savior.

When he attended a national Baptist convention for the first time, David was stirred with a vision of the need to evangelize Brazil. He outlined a plan which he titled, "Every Brazilian Hearing the Gospel." He took the plan to Maddox and told him he would like to present it to the next national convention. Maddox cautioned him that the matter needed more study, but the desire to evangelize Brazil had been planted in David's heart.

For the graduation exercises in 1940, David was to be the valedictory speaker, but he still did not own a Sunday suit. His father, after Franquelina's death, had married Maria Aparecida. They had five children. With so many mouths to feed, Jose had little to spare for new clothes for David. So the two pooled their resources and, at great sacrifice to both, got David a suit. At the commencement service Jose said, "Son, I am proud of you."

A few weeks later a business offer tempted David to try to become a millionaire—to seek money rather than what God wanted for him.

An American, the father of two boys David had helped to care for while in school, owned the Toddy Company, maker of a popular chocolate drink. This man, a native of Puerto Rico, proposed that David head a new enterprise for him, a company to export steel. As an American, the man could not sign all the proper papers for the venture. Thus, he needed a Brazilian as president to do the signing.

"No," David answered. "I plan to be a pastor."

"If you come with me, we will build a church for you as a part of the steel corporation. You can be pastor and won't even have to go to seminary." For the first time, a huge salary dangled before David's longing eyes, like candy before a child. The idea of quick wealth was tantalizing. He struggled to push the thoughts away. That summer the Home Mission Board had invited him to lead evangelistic meetings in the interior. His duty to God was to trust and obey; his answer to the American was no.

Through this decision, David felt that he could identify with Moses who "refused to be called the son of Pharaoh's daughter; choosing rather to suffer affliction with the people of God, than to enjoy the pleasures of sin for a season" (Heb. 11:24-25).

Roads in the interior of Minas in 1940 were mostly nonexistent. Travel was by train, horseback, canoe, or on foot. David spent two months on horseback, riding from place to place.

One tropical night, after preaching, he was returning to the home where he planned to spend the night. His horse galloped at full speed along the trail through the dense forest. Under the closely woven mantle of mighty trees, the earth seemed to have been plunged into blackness.

Now and then the moonlight sifted through the trees in silvery beauty. As David and his horse kept moving mile after mile, the young man noticed that the clouds had begun to thicken. Occasionally he saw flashes of lightning. He urged his horse on, hoping to arrive at his destination before the rain started.

Suddenly David heard a voice call, "Stop!" He pulled back on the reins with all his strength, and the horse obeyed. He got off, wondering what was the matter, and walked cautiously ahead for a few feet. In front of him was a gaping hole, big enough to swallow a horse or break a man's neck. If he had gone on, he would almost certainly have been killed, but he had heard a voice.

David knelt and thanked God. Trusting the Father and him alone for everything was a part of his life, including protection along the dark forest paths.

When at the end of summer David left Minas to enroll at the South Brazil Baptist Seminary in Rio, Maddox gave him a sealed envelope. The letter inside said:

I consider you as one of my own. This letter is similar to ones I have written to my children. You will be going to work in churches where the pastor's daughter is pretty. Remember not to date anyone without thinking first, "Would I want to marry this girl?" You are a young man and you will have temptations as you date. Remember Joseph of Egypt.

5

Haydee, a Present from God

The Lord God said, It is not good that the man should be alone; I will make him an help meet for him (Gen. 2:18).

"You must give her up or give up the seminary." A co-worker at the Baptist Publishing House gave David the ultimatum.

David flung his book down. "I love her, and I will not give her up! I will not give up the seminary! God called me to preach and only God can take me out of the ministry." He stormed out of the building.

Around him the Rio traffic roared and screeched. Bells rang, horns honked, and children laughed, but David paid no attention. If being in love should bring happiness, it had failed to bring him any. Frankly, he was not as sure of himself as he wanted his friends to think.

All along he had convinced himself that because he loved Rosa (not her real name) so much he could persuade her to believe as he believed. For the first time in his life, David was near to admitting defeat.

David had met Rosa in an unusual way. While still in school in Belo, he had made a phone call and dialed a wrong number. Rosa had answered. Intrigued by the conversation, he called her again and continued to call every day.

Rosa in person was even more enchanting than Rosa on the telephone. A blonde, blue-eyed beauty. Well educated, brilliant, studying to be a teacher. Rich. Of high class. Widely read. She could carry on a scintillating conversation on almost any subject. Straightway she captured David's heart.

One flaw marred David's assurance that Rosa would be the perfect wife for him. She had been brought up in a strict Catholic home and believed that only priests should read the Bible. It was not her church affiliation that bothered him, but her failure to realize her need of a new birth in Christ.

At her insistence he studied her religion but still held to his own beliefs. He prayed that she might change, for he could not find the courage to give her up. With misgiving, knowing that he was disobedient to Paul's admonition not to be unequally yoked with an unbeliever, he asked Rosa to marry him.

He left Belo Horizonte in the fall of 1941 to enroll in the South Brazil Baptist Seminary in Rio. With his studies plus two or three jobs, he could sometimes file away the thoughts of Rosa.

As apprentice pastor at the Engenho do Dentro Baptist Church, he assisted the pastor, Richard Pitrawsky. Then Missionary Jack Cowsert asked him if he'd like to work at the Baptist Publishing House.

Even so, he still could only afford one pair of trousers, which he washed on Saturday nights. Often he skipped supper. Some days he broke his breakfast bread into two pieces and saved one slice plus part of his lunch to eat at night.

Fellow students in the dorm made so much noise at night that David would often slip out and sleep beside the back door. From the top of a hill in the Tijuca mountain range, he could see the lights of the city spread far below.

After his discovery of a water fountain in the nearby woods, he adopted the place as his private prayer spot. More and more often he talked with the Lord about the problem in his love life.

Meanwhile during visits to Belo, David continued to see Rosa. By the time of his second year in the seminary, he had spoken with her father, a bank director of Italian descent; a formal engagement announcement had been made.

His employers and friends knew of the engagement. Hence the argument at the publishing house that July day in 1943. After the argument, David was too upset to study or work. He decided to go to Belo to talk with Dona Rosalee. She requested, "Let me meet her. Bring her here and I will talk with her about her need for a personal relationship with Christ." He introduced the two and left them alone together.

Next day he heard Mrs. Appleby's opinion. "She is a marvelous girl, David, a good girl, a wealthy girl, and a cultured girl. But you know, as a pastor you cannot marry her. If she doesn't become a Christian, you would have a most difficult married life."

"But what will I do? I can't give her up!"

"No, you can't, but God can. If it is his will that you give her up, he will help you."

Ready at last for counsel, David realized Dona Rosalee knew what it meant to give up a loved one.

She said, "I want you to do the will of God, whatever that is. If you are following God's directions, don't be afraid of what others will say."

In a place alone, David prayed all night. At last he came to the conviction that he must give up Rosa and the knowledge that God would give him the strength to do it. He asked, "Give me a partner then, Lord, who will encourage and help me to realize the purpose you have for each of us."

As just one more test, he promised God that if Rosa didn't come to any one of four services where he would preach the next week, he would break the engagement. She came to none.

He accepted an invitation to lunch at her house. Her brothers and sisters—doctors, teachers, engineers—were present. After-ward David walked with Rosa in the walled garden; the sky was a cloudless blue beyond the fronds of the palm trees. His heart was painfully heavy as he asked, "Why did you not come to the service last night?" Her answer did not satisfy him.

They spent one more day alone together. David told Rosa, "This is the last time I will come to see you. I loved Jesus before I loved you. He has never betrayed me. I'll keep my word to him."

Telling her parents he was breaking the engagement was the most humiliating moment David had ever faced. Engagement was a serious matter; for according to custom, a young man did not even enter his girl friend's house until after the betrothal.

Dejection stifled his customary lighthearted air after his return to school. Yet he remained determined to let the Lord choose his mate.

That year the Baptist Publishing House sent David to Rio Grande do Sul on a preaching tour. He recorded his impressions of Baptist work in the south for a series of articles for *O Journal Batista.*

This tour included Porto Alegre in the far south, jutting out into the Lagon dos Patos. His hosts in the city were Thelma and Albert Bagby, missionaries on the faculty of Colegio Batista Americana. This school had been started by Albert's sister Alice and her husband Harley Smith and later directed by his sister Helen and her husband W. C. Harrison.

In a tour of the city, they stopped to show David the grave of Albert's father, William Buck Bagby, who had died in Porto Alegre, August 5, 1939. The elder Bagby, a Texan, and his wife, Anne Ellen Luther, had organized the first Brazilian Baptist Church on October 15, 1882. Later, five of their nine children became missionaries to South America.

With Thelma and Albert, David walked down the main thoroughfare, Rua dos Andradas. An icy wind was blowing down from the Andes. Some people, he noted, were wearing woolen *palas*, combination scarf-shawls. David shivered.

"You did not come prepared for the *minuano?*" Albert asked. "I'll lend you a coat."

It was wonderful to get back to the warm "prophet's chamber" that Thelma had assigned him, sip hot maté, and begin his writing. He tried to describe the valley plantations and their grape vineyards, the flat countryside out toward Pelotas, with its grazing cattle, rice and sugar cane, and beyond that orange trees and then the pampas and more cattle. He wrote of the gauchos, the cowboys of the south.

Shortly after he got back to Rio, he received a letter from the Bagbys:

David: You are exactly what we believe a young boy should be (I Timothy 4:12). Although you have been with us so little time it has been enough for us to know that you are one of the rare young men that we would like to keep with us always, eternally. Please remember that we will accompany you in your studies, all your activities, especially this year in deepest intercession.

We look forward with joy to your future career. What wonderful things God has in store for you, because he reserves his choicest blessings for those who give first place to his plan for them. Take with you our prayers and a part of our hearts, the four of us. You have found in us friends for all your life. May God keep you ever.

Thelma, Albert, Danny, and Albert, Jr.

David had confided to Thelma his turmoil over the breakup with Rosa. She tried to mend his heart with a girl named Gabriela, but the intended matchmaking did not work out.

One afternoon in September, 1944, a demure, dark-haired girl dropped by the Baptist Publishing House to deliver some cards from a young people's contest in her hometown of Curitiba. Quietly she handed the cards to David and left. She was like a butterfly, alighting briefly then flying away.

"That's Haydee Suman," another worker spoke up. "She's a student at the Baptist Training School. They say she's consecrated and capable—and I would add lovable! You should marry her!"

David thought the girl charming but gave her no more thought just then. Graduation time was nearing and his thesis was not completed.

An unpleasant happening had occurred at the school. David's knowledge of the affair was not enough that he could see the matter objectively. Like his father, David often talked too much. He gave a biased account in his thesis. The paper was rejected. Thus, he was told he could not graduate, in spite of his top grades.

Not knowing what else to do, David prayed. He asked God to guide him in the choice of a Bible passage that would contain a message from him. In the thirteenth chapter of John, David read about Jesus' washing the disciples' feet. Perhaps he needed to be less critical and more humble. Maybe he should rewrite the thesis as the professor wanted it written. All night he worked on the necessary changes.

"You did it all again?" the astonished professor asked. This time the paper was accepted, and David was appointed to deliver the graduation speech for his class. Among the seniors at the Training School, Haydee Suman had been chosen valedictorian.

At graduation time it was traditional for the seminary and the training school to stage a joint farewell festival or *saudade*. Such a farewell party, held outdoors on November 27, 1944, turned out to be one of the most important events of David's life.

Three young men in his class and he stood near the front of the seminary chapel talking about finding a girl to marry. One of the others showed a picture of Haydee Suman and said he planned to win her. The other two agreed she was a fine girl, worthy of courting, truly talented, and remarkable.

For once, David was listening and not talking. He made not a single comment, but silently resolved, "I will get her!" He recalled an old saying from his native state: "People from Minas Gerais don't talk. They get, after a time of silence."

As the line formed for refreshments on the cobblestone plaza in the L of the seminary buildings, David saw the slender Haydee in the line and realized how lovely she was. He walked over to stand beside her, leaned close, and whispered, "Would you marry me?"

"No," she retorted. Determination in her expressive brown eyes, she looked up at him. "I am not thinking of marriage. I plan to be a missionary in the interior of Brazil." *Her rich, throaty voice is nice,* he thought, *and her brown hair has a slight auburn tint.*

Someone was playing a love song on a mandolin, and David could not take no for an answer. When Haydee was ready to leave, he walked with her along the mosaic sidewalk to the bus stop. Above the babble of the traffic, he told her, "I'll be waiting for you to say yes."

Haydee Suman had grown up in Parana. Coming from this state in south Brazil where Germans and Italians and other European colonists had settled, she had an educational and cultural background that most from other parts of the country in her student days did not have.

Her grandparents had all lived and died in south Italy. Her mother, nominally a Catholic, actually had no practicing religion. Haydee, until she was thirteen, attended the Presbyterian church in Curitiba with her father and sisters. Yet she had felt like a boat without direction. She had begun to feel she had no need for any church so she quit going at all.

Then at seventeen she realized she was wasting her life working against God. She enrolled in a Baptist Sunday School class taught by Mrs. Ben Oliver, who had been a missionary to Italy before transferring to Brazil. Listening to Mrs. Oliver's teachings and studying the Bible for herself, Haydee realized her need for a

Savior. Her conversion experience changed the direction of her life.

Haydee's mother did not approve of her baptism in the Baptist church by Pastor Joao Emilio Henck. Because of her mother's attitude, Haydee moved to Rio to live with her sister Carmen. There she enrolled in the Baptist Training School.

W. E. and Edith Allen, a missionary couple on the Training School faculty, were delighted when Haydee volunteered for mission service, for she was one of their favorite students. Then David Gomes came along and spoiled their plans.

David's father, however, encouraged him to continue wooing Haydee. "That girl has a sweet face. She will be a good wife."

After graduation David was called as co-pastor of the Thomas Coelho (Thomas Rabbit) Church where Cowsert was pastor. For David's ordination to the ministry on December 1, 1944, thirty-one pastors and several deacons served on the examining council, the largest such council until that time. Among the men were A. R. Crabtree, president of the South Brazil Seminary; W. C. Taylor, theologian; Reynaldo Purin, seminary professor; and Manoel Avelino de Souze.

Three weeks later, on his twenty-fifth birthday, December 23, 1944, David traveled to Curitiba to ask Haydee for her final answer.

She told him, "The night of the party I did not sleep at all. I kept asking the Lord, 'Can it be?' I had two problems. My mother was saying no to my desire to be a missionary, and Bratcher was waiting for me to say when I would be ready to go to the field. Then you added another problem. Would I marry you? Well, David, my answer to you is yes."

That day they announced the engagement. Her mother was happy, but Bratcher was disappointed.

The Allens were incredulous when David and Haydee visited them. "Are you sure this is the right decision?" Mrs. Allen asked.

David brashly interrupted: "She will do more for missions as my wife than she would as a missionary."

He was more a prophet than he realized. Could he know that one day Haydee would be president of Brazil's Foreign Mission Board, serve with him as collaborator in a nationwide radio program, and write a column for the Baptist journal? Could he know that she would be a leader of Brazilian Baptist women—and perhaps more important—rear six children, all dedicated to the Lord and missions, at home and abroad? David did know Haydee shared his longing "that all the world might know."

Before David proposed, Christians at Curitiba who had heard him preach wrote Haydee, praising him. She had read the articles he wrote in Porto Alegre for *O Jornal Batista*. After he proposed, she reread them.

The wedding was set for August 11, 1945, Haydee's birthday, at First Baptist Church of Curitiba. She asked Pastor Henck, who had baptized her, to perform the ceremony.

In July a group of Baptists were enroute from Rio to a convention in Vitoria, 260 miles to the northeast. A new missionary, Dorine Hawkins (Stewart), was among the passengers who sat packed together on wooden benches in the old, wood-burning train; the open windows let the air and hot cinders in. David talked to Dorine above the noise of the wheels, in English because he was anxious to practice.

"Haydee and I will be married in August," he told her. "We have been accepted as students at Southwestern Seminary in Texas." Then he added, "I want you to know that after my salvation I consider Haydee the greatest present God could have given me."

From the port of Paranagua a remarkable railroad winds up over a mountain range to Curitiba, a large and modern city. The railroad crosses deep gorges and streams full of boulders.

From the train the traveler can see bamboo and banana trees, and miles of giant parana pines with their slender trunks and top branches stretching out on each side. But the scenery from the sea to Curitiba is no more beautiful than was the First Baptist Church of Curitiba on Haydee's wedding day.

Members of the church had gathered 240 dozen velvety white calla lilies, called "glasses of milk." With these, they decorated the sanctuary. Haydee wore a long white dress and carried a bouquet of flowers arranged by her sister Angela. In the beauty of the lilies she and David exchanged their vows.

6

The Southwestern Baptist Theological Seminary

Study to shew thyself approved unto God, a workman that needeth not to be ashamed, rightly dividing the word of truth (2 Tim. 2:15).

"They don't have any tickets left," David told Jack Cowsert, "but I don't have enough money to buy their tickets anyway."

"Lack of money is not your problem!" the missionary countered. "The problem is that you did not listen to me and make the reservations on the ship."

"The agent said he would add our names to the waiting list and that maybe we could get tickets within the next seven months."

"Seven months! The school year will be practically over by then."

At Mrs. Appleby's suggestion and Cowsert's urging, David and Haydee had decided to go to Fort Worth to study religious education at Southwestern Baptist Theological Seminary.

There would be difficulties to overcome, one of the main ones being the cost. However, with a firm disposition as always to follow God's divine will, David left the matter to him. He did not know all of God's plan for him, but in faith he had surrendered his life. If the Lord wanted him to go to the States, he reasoned, the obstacles would be removed.

One desire consumed him—that all the people of Brazil might know Christ. He wanted to spend his life telling as many people as possible the news that Jesus loved them. He wanted to tell everybody in the world, but he would begin first with Brazil. If studying in the United States would make him a more effective witness, then that was what he wanted to do.

In late summer of 1945, World War II was drawing to a close and tickets for ocean travel were still hard to get. More than once Cowsert reminded David to reserve space with the Delta Line, but he stubbornly repeated that if God wanted him to go he would work out the arrangements.

56

Mrs. Appleby had written E. D. Head, the president of Southwestern Baptist Theological Seminary, so a job waited for David at the seminary. Baptist Women in Yazoo County, Mississippi, had established a scholarship for him. People from Crystal Springs and other towns in Mississippi and Texas had given to a fund for his education.

Now it was nearly time for the boat to leave, but David had no tickets or reservations. Faced with these facts, the young man said to Cowsert, "If God doesn't want me to go, I don't want to go. If it is God's will, a door will open."

David and Haydee lived in an apartment on Governor's Island among many old trees, fruit vendors, and little shops. Sometimes when they rode the bus that circled the island, they got off at a sweet shop by the beach and shared a lemonade.

At that time, the bridge had not been built to the island. One night David had to wait for the ferry a long time and was extremely late getting home. Since they had only been married a few weeks, he thought Haydee would be waiting up, worried. She was asleep. Next morning she told him she knew he was in the Lord's work, so she need not worry.

Shortly the Delta Line notified David of a cancellation which had made a stateroom available on a freighter, "if you can leave tomorrow."

He called Haydee to ask, "Can you start packing now?"

The next day they left Brazil. All the money he had saved would not have been enough to pay half the fare on the ship Cowsert had designated. Passage on the freighter for the two of them cost ten thousand cruzeiros, exactly the amount David had saved for the tickets.

As the ship exited Rio harbor, the couple stood on deck to bid farewell for awhile to Governor's Island, the Sugar Loaf, and the curving sand beaches. Even before the statue on Corcovado had disappeared in the distance, David had taken out his notebook and jotted down three goals he hoped to reach while in the States.

At least two of the goals, he felt, would bring him nearer his goal to win Brazil for Christ. First, he wanted to speak at First Baptist Church of Dallas because it was the largest Baptist church in the

world and because he so much admired George Truett. Second, he
wanted to speak in chapel at the seminary. Third, he wanted to
speak at the Southern Baptist Convention.

Twenty-one days later David and Haydee disembarked. Soon
they got their first glimpse of Seminary Hill, treeless then under the
wide Texas sky. They moved into a room in Fort Worth Hall.

David didn't wait for a perfect command of the English language before he tried to communicate with his new friends. He just
started talking, correct or not. Haydee was more quiet and intense
in her practice of English.

When David reported to work in the seminary cafeteria, the
manager assigned him the task of serving bread. He told her he
didn't know much about American bread.

"When they ask for brown bread, give them this; when they
ask for white bread, give them this."

One student asked for heels. David had never heard of heels
to eat, so he had to ask where the heels were kept. Another student
asked for light bread. David conferred again with his boss to find out
that *white* and *light* meant the same in reference to bread.

In the same way, he learned that whole bread was the same as
brown bread. Because he responded with good humor, students
liked to kid him and kept trying to confuse him with the many types
of bread. Eventually he learned that the heels were good dipped in
the juice of pinto beans. His daily food budget, for himself and
Haydee, was $1.50, so this, he found, was a good, inexpensive
lunch or supper.

Various professors invited the Brazilian couple to visit in their
homes—President Head, W. T. Conner, J. M. Price, T. B. Mas-
ton, Ray Summers, Frank Means.

Innately courteous, they wanted to send thank-you notes. Following meals at several professors' homes and homes of others,
they began to send sympathy cards to their hosts. Did not *sym-
pathia* in Portuguese express warmest feelings? And warmest
expressions of thanks were what they wished to send.

When they discovered the extent of their error, they decided it
was time to take some private English lessons. Bob Hastings, a
classmate, offered to tutor them in grammar and composition for a

small fee. Hastings had been attracted to David's ever-present smile as he handed out the bread.

Interested in translating theological textbooks into Portuguese for the benefit of Brazilian pastors, David started "The Portuguese Translation Fund." When he spoke in a church, as he did almost every Sunday, the congregation often gave an offering to his fund. Hastings felt that the fund had merit and human interest, so he interviewed David and wrote an article about it for the *Brotherhood Journal.*

Other friends David made in the cafeteria line were Jack Mac-Gorman and Ruth Stephens. He'd been constantly watching the two, looking first into the eyes of one and then the other to discern the signs of love. So far, he wasn't satisfied with the progress the couple was making. Something ought to be done to help those two along!

The next time he saw them enter the crowded cafeteria, he held up his left hand and pointed to his ring finger. "The ring, Jack?" he called out. "Where's the ring?"

Both Jack and Ruth turned several shades of red. Without admitting it to each other, they rather enjoyed the impetuous urging of the brother from Brazil. Later, when they sat down at the table with Haydee, she tried to smooth things over by explaining that David had asked her to become his wife even before they had gone out on a date. Later in the year Jack did give Ruth a ring.

David's other job involved cleaning the dorms. On the freight elevator one day, he reached for the brake and grabbed the wrong rope. His hands were burned so badly that he had to be taken to the emergency room at the hospital. In this experience, he felt the warm caring of Christian friends for strangers from another land.

David and Haydee found another friend in their pastor at Broadway Church, Forrest Feezor. At the time, the liquor question was an inflammatory issue in Fort Worth. One Sunday Feezor ended his sermon against the evils of alcohol with the statement, "If there is a member of this church who is in the liquor business, I think he ought to give up the business or give up the church."

David was impressed with Feezor's stand for the right, regardless of consequences to self. He resolved to make it a practice in his own ministry always to stand for what he believed to be right, no matter the cost.

When he got an invitation to speak to a Woman's Missionary Union meeting at First Baptist Church of Dallas, he was so excited he could not keep still. He had already reached his first goal!

David refused a request to speak at First Baptist Church, Houston, however, because he already had an engagement at a mission in Denton. While in Denton, he and Haydee were eating at a cafe. A large woman with a wide smile came over and asked, "What strange language is that you are talking?"

"Portuguese." They introduced themselves.

"I am Kathleen Henderson, First Baptist Church."

Just before Christmas, they returned to Denton to find the Sunday School assembly room decorated with candles and poinsettias and a new loudspeaker system set up and in use. Mrs. Henderson said, "Brother Gomes, this loudspeaker is for you to take back to Brazil." It was from the class she taught, the Fidelis Matrons Class.

At the seminary, Missions Day came on a Friday. Dann and Doris Sharpley had planned to skip chapel and get an early start to their church field a hundred miles away. But Doris put her foot down. David Gomes was to be the speaker in chapel, and she was staying to hear him.

In chapel, every seat was taken. The foyer outside was jammed with people. A sense of expectancy was in the atmosphere. Doris and Dann arrived a little late and had to sit on the back row in the balcony.

Before coming to the seminary, Dann had been in the navy and had been stationed in Brazil for nearly four years. He had learned to love Brazil and Brazilians. During World War II, in military service in Rio, he had felt God was calling him to preach. After a transfer back to the States, Dann was discharged and enrolled at the seminary.

There he met Doris Allred Woodrum and David and Haydee Gomes. Immediately, David began pressing Dann to go back to Brazil as a missionary. Dann explained that he felt called to preach, but not in Brazil. David would not be deterred. Sometimes Dann was so annoyed, he was not even polite. In the meantime, he married Doris and accepted a weekend church field.

At chapel that morning, David told about opportunities for spreading the gospel message in Brazil. Then he made an impassioned appeal for students to dedicate their lives to missions.

Though the Sharpleys were sitting at the top of the balcony, the Spirit of the Lord reached them. He used David Gomes to touch their hearts. Suddenly Dann no longer felt so sure that God was not calling him to Brazil. He looked at his wife and saw expectation in her eyes. Instantly both knew this was it.

Dann and Doris walked from the top of the balcony to the front of the auditorium to dedicate their lives. They had no children yet. Dann knew a little Portuguese. He could find no reason why they should not go.

In the same service, James Musgrave also surrendered for mission service in Brazil.

David knew now there had been a valid reason for his desire to speak in seminary chapel. His second goal had been reached.

It appeared that his goal to speak at the Southern Baptist Convention might not be realized. Then he got a letter from Theron Rankin, inviting him to speak on foreign missions night at the 1947 convention in Saint Louis.

When David got off the train in Saint Louis, he was told that all hotels in the city were full. Consequently, he spent the night on a bench in the railroad station, engulfed in the aroma of stale tobacco smoke and tired, unwashed travelers.

At the registration booth next day, David met Thomas Clinkscales, a missionary to Brazil, who helped him find a place to stay.

In his convention message, David gave his testimony. He thanked Southern Baptists for what their missions efforts had meant to him. Again he used the chance to ask for more missionaries to his country. Afterward he was invited to preach at First Baptist Church, Richmond, Virginia. For the first time, he had an opportunity to go to Washington, DC, where he met Baptist World Alliance leaders.

His visits to New Mexico were significant. After he spoke at Camp Inlow, the Woman's Missionary Union of New Mexico gave him a jeep. Then at Clovis, New Mexico, he and Haydee visited Mr. and Mrs. Robert Stone and met the relatives of Ray Buster and her sister, Ione.

Since David could not yet drive, Mrs. Stone and her friend, Mrs. W. H. Vaughter, took the couple for a ride in the new jeep. David's elation was sky-high, for he knew the jeep would be great for his use on the rough roads in rural Brazil.

At Clovis, David spoke at Central Baptist Church. Then he was dramatically escorted to the meeting room of the Lydia Class. Hanging on the wall was a picture of him as a young boy in the suit borrowed from Missionary Riffey and stuffed with newspaper. At last, he was told that the Lydia Class and Robert Stone had been his mysterious benefactors during his high school years.

To see that picture again, hanging on the wall of a church, touched his heart. David stood looking at it with the tears rolling down his cheeks.

7

Seventeen Preaching Points

The spirit lifted me up and took me away to Tel Abib, another colony of Jewish exiles beside the Chebar River. I went in bitterness and anger, but the hand of the Lord was strong upon me. And I sat among them, overwhelmed, for seven days (Ezek. 3:14-15, TLB).

The Rio *favela* had no resemblance to the common wildflower for which it was named. Houses were not really houses—just jumbles of rooms thrown together with scraps of old lumber, cardboard, and rusted tin.

Halfway up the 800-foot hill, David and two young men stopped to rest. Ahead of them, a woman struggled upward with two heavy cans of water she'd lugged from the bottom of the hill. Beside them lay the ruins of a shanty that had slid down the mountainside in a rainstorm.

"What do you want?" an unshaven man asked. Before David could open his mouth to answer, two drunkards lunged out of a house, their knives aimed with the intent to kill.

The surprise attack so scared David that he turned and ran up the hill, winding through the muddy alleyways with record speed. Behind him, an assailant hit one of David's companions in the face, but otherwise all three got away unhurt. David went on and performed the duty he was assigned to do.

Next morning a newspaper printed David's picture with the headline, "Courageous Pastor Escapes Death."

David's diligence for witnessing in the slums had nearly cost him his life that Sunday afternoon. At the time of this escapade, he was pastor of the Tijuca Baptist Church in Rio.

"Let nothing keep you from Minas," O. P. Maddox had advised him, and David had fully intended to follow that advice.

Then a letter from the Tijuca Church caused him to hesitate. A. R. Crabtree, a missionary pastor, was in poor health and needed to reduce his responsibilities. The church wanted David to become the pastor when he graduated from seminary. In the meantime, the letter said, Missionary Hafford Berry would continue as interim pastor.

"Let nothing keep you from Minas" kept echoing in his mind until David traveled to Waco to talk with Maddox. This visit, plus much praying, led David to accept the call to Tijuca.

After he and Haydee got their Master of Religious Education degrees in Fort Worth, they moved to Rio in February, 1948. The church in the foothills of the Tijuca mountain range was then thirty years old and had around two hundred members.

Middle-class homes of the Tijuca area mingled with elegant houses that had walled courtyards and iron grillwork over the windows, plus flowering trees and vines in abundance. Above these were the *favelas,* the slums on the precarious slopes of the city's hills.

In the beginning of *favelas,* squatters would slip onto a piece of unoccupied land and throw up a few huts, often at night. Then the owner of the land could remove them only by taking legal action.

As David looked up at night at the shacks, lighted by kerosene lamps or the lower ones by electricity, he longed to reach out to the people to tell them of Jesus' love.

David's evangelistic zeal was infectious. Since the South Brazil Baptist Seminary and Girls' Training School were not far, some of the students and faculty were members of the Tijuca Chruch. These and other church members, especially young people, made up evangelism teams to preach and sing and conduct Sunday Schools in the *favelas.* Before long, the church had seventeen preaching points.

Up and down the hills, David visited the church members and made friends with people in the slums near the mission points. His time at home grew less and less.

As a rule, Haydee was patient, but she didn't mind giving her opinion. One day she called David and said, "If you continue in the way you are doing, it would be better if you just take your bed and sleep in the slums!"

He listened and knew she was right. Yet, in intense empathy for the *favela* dwellers, he could project himself into their place and feel their physical and spiritual poverty. Once he had been poor, so he could identify with them.

David was teaching the young people to be soul-winners. At the same time, they were learning to reach out through the preaching points. One afternoon the teenage daughter of a deacon was one of those who went with David to visit a *favela* home.

After they had returned, the girl started crying. She said, "I have to confess my sins to Jesus. I am ashamed because at my house I never accept only beans and rice. I was touched by the way the girl we visited was happy to have some beans and rice to eat." That day David understood better Ezekiel 3:14-15.

David told a colleague, "The power of our witnessing is our capacity to identify with the persons to whom we give the message of the gospel."

During the first months back in Rio, Haydee filled her days with shopping at the street markets, working in church duties, cooking, and keeping house. She was pregnant with their first child.

In the kitchen, she often had her husband's help. Since the days when he learned to cook after his mother's death he had enjoyed showing his culinary prowess. If dinner were not ready when he got home, he didn't complain, but prepared the meal.

In the mornings, David would occasionally walk to the nearby bakery in his house shoes to buy bread to go with his butter for breakfast. With his Brazilian sweet tooth, he liked syrup and *farinha* over sausages and bread. He began his day with the usual small cup of very black, very sweet coffee, "black as midnight, strong as love, hot as fire."

David tried their new gadget from America, the Presto cooker. As the whistling started, he grabbed the pot and opened it without waiting for it to cool. Beans exploded in his face, stuck to his cheeks, nose, head, neck, and arms. The burns were severe, but they left no scars.

From the very first days of their marriage, Haydee realized that she and her husband had different points of view about many things. She had plans for a beautiful home, nice furniture, everything in its right place. None of these were on David's mind. He only planned to have a church, to be a preacher, to get all the instruction he could in how to make God known to people.

Material things were not of particular importance to him. If he got them, that was fine; if he did not, he did not lose any sleep because of it. For the church, he did not mind making appeals for money; but for self, he did not like to spend money on nonessentials. Superfluous items were not in his budget.

Haydee found out too that she had married a happy man, full of ideas and ideals, who really believed that no obstacle was too difficult for God to remove. Most people said they believed God was all-powerful, but David acted like he believed it. He never stopped talking, except when he fell asleep. One day she told him, "It's a good thing God made me your wife. I like to hear more than to talk!"

The church grew as David's enthusiastic preaching and Bible teaching drew more listeners. The Wednesday night prayer service became a time no one wanted to miss.

As the church grew, so did the pastor's family. Ana Maria was born August 6, 1948. That night Sophia Nichols and Olga Berry rode to the hospital with Haydee and David. When Sophia had come as a missionary to Rio the preceding year, she had joined the Tijuca Church. Olga and Hafford Berry had also continued to be members.

Late in the night, David saw his baby daughter for the first time. Then all the way home he sang hymns, as Olga listened. He was so happy he could not be silent one second.

Training young people to be soul-winners, David knew, would be a key to winning all Brazil for Christ. The young choir gave concerts in the open air so multitudes could hear. A Volunteer Band was organized for young people who surrendered to full-time Christian service.

Training young preachers was important; they needed a thorough knowledge of the Bible. To have contact with young preachers, David started teaching a night class in theology at the South Brazil Seminary. In addition, the church allowed him two months a year to preach in revivals in other churches; he stretched that to three months by adding his month's vacation time.

Along with approval of the Tijuca pastor came some dissatis-faction with him. David was an individualist who had his own way of doing things, and this sometimes attracted criticism. However, criticism didn't stop David from doing what he felt God wanted him to do or preaching the message he believed God had given him.

One young man confided to the pastor, "A deacon, a charter member, is angry with you and may cause problems in the church." When David heard the jokes the deacon had been telling about him, he sought a time to talk with the man privately. David was not afraid of misunderstandings but liked to go straight to the heart of them, openly and honestly. His letter to the deacon got no reply.

Finally one day when David saw the man alone, he told him, "Your attitude is the reason all your children are out of the church, lost." At this, the man broke down and began to cry. It turned into a time of spiritual victory for both men, a time of healing, and a begin-ning of friendship. Later, most of the deacon's children became active Christians in the church.

Before David moved to Tijuca, the church had bought some property which, after some consideration, appeared too small for the church's building needs.

David asked Alberto Mazoni, an engineer, to study the possi-blity of enlarging the existing auditorium. Mazoni told the church there was plenty of space at the rear to double the seating capacity with an annex. Within three months, the addition was ready for use.

In the six years of David's Tijuca pastorate, the number of members tripled to six hundred. Ninety percent of those were tithers. Two more babies were born to Haydee and David at Tijuca. Priscila arrived August 10, 1950. A son, Marcos David, made his appearance March 3, 1953.

And a child was born to the church, a radio program called the "Bible School of the Air."

8

Bible School of the Air

Faith cometh by hearing, and hearing by the word of God (Rom. 10:17).

Halfway between Pelotas and Santa Maria the aged black Ford started making funny noises. As it rattled into Cachoeira do Sul, it skipped a time or two, backfired, and quit. Its occupants were not ones who let car trouble frustrate them.

Soon the two had settled the details to have the car repaired. Then they followed the scent of sizzling beef to a churrasco restaurant. They sat, mouths watering, at an outdoor table and watched the cooks roast great chunks of beef on a spit over a bed of red hot coals. A waiter delivered meat still on a spit, to their table. With a long razor-sharp knife, he cut off thick, juicy slices and laid them on the plates.

Exercise and the outdoor air had made both of them hungry. They attacked the meat with fervor, while they rehashed old times at the seminary. They had heard the gauchos say they never ate nuts and bananas, but always started the day with two kilos of mutton and beef. After this meal, they could believe it. David had spoken at a meeting in Pelotas and was on the way home with Dann Sharpley to preach at his church at Santa Maria. Dann and Doris had been missionaries in Rio Grande do Sul for a year; David was still pastor at Tijuca.

"I hear your church has a radio program," Dann said. "How's it going?"

"We started with five minutes. Now we've gone to ten."

A Rio station had invited the Tijuca Church to do a brief weekly program, as a sort of public service. For the first one, on a Saturday, Pastor Gomes gave a short commentary on the Sunday School lesson. Letters of approval came in, so he continued the Bible study format.

A correspondence course was added for shut-ins and for the

Extension Department of the Sunday School, plus other interested listeners.

In a Sunday School teachers' meeting at the church, a teacher said, "Our radio program is like a school."

Another added, "Then let's call it the 'Bible School of the Air.' "

Now Dann asked, "You're going to continue the questions and answers about the Bible?"

"Yes, that has been well received."

"But why limit your audience? You could go on a larger station with shortwave broadcasting and be heard all over the country."

After they finished eating, David and Dann continued to sit and talk and listen to the cafe's radio. During a break in the music, an announcer identified the station as Radio Tamoio of Rio.

There they sat in Rio Grande do Sul, hearing music from a thousand miles to the north. They were in a city of thirty thousand that had no Baptist church, no gospel message as Baptists preach it.

"David! Do you hear that? Get your program on a station like that and you can reach all of Brazil for Christ."

That day toward the end of 1949, the "Bible School of the Air" really got off the ground. Later, as the two men drove on to Santa Maria, David got more and more excited about the possibilities. Before he left Dann and Doris' house, he was convinced that God was leading him to take the program to Radio Tamoio. If he had the faith to try, he knew God would be his partner to accomplish what seemed to him impossible.

He didn't stop to worry about how one church could pay for such a program or where the money might come from. He just took God at his word—"Go . . . and teach . . . and lo, I am with you." The idea of how many people could tune in to those radio waves had struck David like lightning. How many would hear, who had never before heard, that Jesus loved them?

Back home in Rio, David found a letter from Kathleen Henderson. She and the Fidelis Sunday School Class of Denton had sent a check for fifty dollars, to use as needed. Immediately he drove to Radio Tamoio and asked to speak to the station director.

"He is not here."

"I'll wait."

"He won't be here until three this afternoon."

"I don't want to miss him. I'll wait."

The receptionist tried to discourage David. She told him the station never aired Protestant programs.

At three, David told the director, "I want to teach Bible lessons on your station."

"We never broadcast anything concerning the Bible."

"My program will never criticize other religions or denominations. We will just preach the plain gospel message from the Bible."

"All right," he said. "I'll let you have fifteen minutes a week, but you must pay." He named a number of cruzeiros, the equivalent of thirty dollars.

"I can pay."

"You need a sponsor," the manager said, "as your guarantor that the pay will come in weekly."

"God is sponsor for all my programs."

Finally the director conceded, "I've never transacted radio business with God, but we will give it a try."

David wrote and recorded the scripts for the programs. He was publicity man and agent as well. He devised a "Bible School of the Air" banner: an open Bible and radio tower against a green and white background. Postcards were printed with the banner and Romans 10:17, the Bible school Scripture, "Faith cometh by hearing, and hearing by the word of God."

The banner meant "circling the world with the Gospel": green for hope; white for purity; blue for promises; red, the blood of Christ; and yellow, riches in Christ. Beams from the tower were yellow, the lettering was red, and the edges of the Bible, blue.

As David told his radio audience, "Faith is a seed." As a seed sprouts and grows, so did the "Bible School of the Air" grow. The number of stations carrying the program and the number of letters from listeners slowly but steadily increased.

Trusting God for everything had become a way of life for David. Day by day he relied upon God to supply the financial needs for the radio broadcasts. It was a faith ministry that was not in the church budget. Tijuca Church contributed to it, beyond the church's gifts to the Cooperative Program and other missions gifts. The church in Denton, Texas, continued to send regular monthly contributions. Listeners spontaneously sent offerings, as did other churches. Always, just enough came to meet the immediate bills— rarely too much or too little.

In 1953, the program was registered as a legal entity with its own bylaws and a Bible school board was elected, made up of Brazilian Baptist pastors and laymen.

In December, 1953, David was in Curitiba to preach at the National Youth Congress when he heard on his own radio program that Lewis Bratcher had died. How well he remembered one sermon Bratcher had preached in Belo!

Through tears, he shared the news with the young people, then spoke on the text, Ecclesiastes 11:1, "Cast thy bread upon the waters," applying it to Bratcher's life.

The following month, as vice-president of the Home Mission Board, David read Bratcher's last written report during the meeting of the Brazilian Baptist Convention.

Lewis Bratcher had been the "pioneer for Christ," "the hero of the interior," the executive secretary of the Brazilian Baptist Home Mission Board for twenty-seven years. The Home Mission Board chose a nominating committee to search for another executive secretary and appointed David as its chairman.

Suggestions of names were mailed to the committee, but no name seemed to be the right one. The committee continued to pray. A letter from a home missionary in Bahia suggested the name of David Gomes. David read the letter but did not tell the other committee members.

Finally, on March 13, 1954, the president of the Board, Jose de Miranda Pinto, who had been on his knees for a long time, stood up and asked, "Tell me, Brother Gomes, is there another letter not yet presented to us?"

"Yes."

"Who is the person it suggests?"

"Myself."

Then Pinto exclaimed, "You are the secretary!"

David wanted to pray more about the matter of accepting such a nomination. For four days he stayed in Sao Vicente, preaching in T. C. Bagby's church. While there, he decided to accept the job if elected.

T. C. Bagby, another son of Anne and William Buck Bagby, was so elated over David's nomination that he gave him one of his most treasured books, a gift from his wife, *10,000 Biblical Illustrations*. In it he wrote, "Presented to my colleague, David Gomes, during the conference held in our church at Sao Vicente, May, 1954."

June 12, 1954, David was elected the Home Mission Board executive secretary, at age thirty-four. Twenty of twenty-one votes had been cast for him. The Board member who didn't vote for him was a deacon at Tijuca Church who hated to lose his pastor.

Part II

The Tree: 1949-1969

9

To Win Brazil for Christ

Ye shall be witnesses unto me . . . in all Judea (Acts 1:8).

At the corner of Barao de Mesquita Street, a traffic signal had gone dead. As David entered the intersection, another car banged into his jeep so hard it flipped over three times. When he woke up at the city hospital in Rio, he asked, "Where is the money?"

David had been on the way to the downtown post office to mail the home missionaries their salaries. As usual, he hurried, though groggy from lack of sleep.

When he began his duties as executive secretary of the Home Mission Board, not enough money was left in the budget to pay all the missionaries' salaries. Minnie Landrum, red-haired missionary from Mississippi and executive secretary of the Woman's Missionary Union of Brazil, allowed him to use some undesignated funds from the WMU to meet the payroll that month.

Immediately David placed the money in a briefcase. Then, as a protective measure, he asked a man on his office staff to ride in the jeep with him to the post office. Then came the crash.

"Where is the money?" David asked. His co-worker had rescued the briefcase.

"If you lose your ring, you still have your finger." That old proverb was certainly true in his case. His jeep was ruined; but he was not badly hurt himself, and no one had stolen the money. Afterward, women from New Mexico sent him a car to replace the jeep.

The Home Mission Board had been organized in 1907 at the suggestion of Solomon Ginsburg, a Southern Baptist missionary. Five Brazilians and five Southern Baptist missionaries had headed it in the first twenty years.

Then, from 1926 until his death twenty-seven years later, Lewis Bratcher had been executive secretary. Though he never

became a real master of the Portuguese language, Bratcher loved
Brazilians, and they loved him. As a pioneer, he had led Baptists to
establish work in the valleys of the Araguaia, Tocantins, and Sao
Francisco Rivers. At the time of his death, the Board projects included one theological institute, three medical dispensaries, a mission farm, twenty-eight primary schools, and about a hundred missionaries. These were supported by the few but generous resources
furnished by Brazilian Baptists.

"Who can possibly replace Bratcher?" people asked. His suc-
cessor, David Gomes, was able to accomplish what some had
thought impossible—maintain what had been started by Bratcher,
and at the same time, expand the work.

In the early days, deficits in the budget were common. Eco-
nomic depression and devaluation of the national money caused
problems. But gradually the amount of the special missions offerings climbed. Also Brazilian Baptists organized a Cooperative Program patterned after Southern Baptists' program of finance. This
brought a more even and steady flow of financial aid to home missions.

The evangelistic fervor that marked David's Tijuca pastorate
did not dwindle when he got into the work of home missions. He
wanted to do in the whole country what he had tried to do in the
slums of Rio—tell as many as possible as fast as possible about the
love of Jesus.

He adopted the slogan, "To Win Brazil for Christ." A column
he began in O Jornal Batista was called "The March of Home Missions."

The first year, he could not go everywhere fast enough to suit
himself. He wanted to travel into all parts of the country, to encourage the missionaries, to seek out new needs, to preach in revivals,
to check on the needs of the institutions, and to witness personally
to as many as he could wherever he happened to be.

Eventually he did visit every state, every territory, every capital, and most of the small towns and cities, in the whole country.
This was quite a feat in a country 2,690 miles wide and 2,670 miles
long at the farthest point from north to south.

When there was no hotel, David slept on a hammock slung

under the back of a truck, in a boarding house, or in any home where he could find shelter. In cities, he never chose a first-class hotel but always a middle-class one so he could save the mission money.

He had accepted the Home Mission Board post in the understanding that he could continue working with the radio programs. Often while riding, he would write his sermons or radio scripts. He practiced economy in everything. Stories and sermons were written on the back side of waste paper.

As David traveled to the different sections of the country, he opened preaching points, especially along the rivers and new roads under construction. Later these became churches. He searched for the best locations for new schools and medical clinics. When possible, the Home Mission Board sent missionaries to these villages.

Often in small towns, David could find no food for sale. At one time, during the dry season, he could find no vegetables or fruits so he bought some sausages which he boiled in a can of water.

One difficulty followed another, but to him they did not seem hard. He accepted things as they were. He was never alone, for the Lord always traveled with him and provided for him a place to sleep and something to eat.

In the 1950s, few roads reached into the interior. How to get anywhere was a continuing puzzle. David rode horses, small planes, buses, burros, ox carts, trains, jeeps, canoes, and riverboats. Often he walked. Sometimes he climbed onto big trucks loaded with beans, corn, or rice. Often he saw people clinging to the tops of loaded freight trucks on their way to the cities to try to find jobs and improve their standard of living.

From the steaming waterlogged Amazon jungle to the scrubby deserts of the northeast, from the coffee plantations of Parana to the sugarcane fields of Pernambuco, from the wild jacaranda forests of the Mato Grosso to the pampas of Rio Grande do Sul, from the old mining towns of Minas to the gigantic, cosmopolitan Sao Paulo, David marveled at the staggering variety of landscapes in his country.

David talked with jangadeiros who went to sea on balsam rafts outfitted with sails. He met the rough-looking but softhearted vaqueros, or cowboys, of Piaui, and the gauchos, the cowboys of the far south. He made friends with European immigrants in Santa Catarina. And he camped with Indians far from civilization.

Along the banks of the Amazon, when his boat stopped at a cluster of huts, some on stilts, David went ashore to talk with the residents of the huts. Swarms of children clustered around him as he told them entertaining Bible stories and taught them songs about Jesus.

The ocean river, as the Indians called it, changed from olive green to yellow to chocolate brown, depending on the sky and the amount of mud under the water.

On one occasion, the ship David rode was as full of luggage and livestock—hens, pigs, goats—as it was of people. They met big timber carriers and fishermen's canoes made of logs scooped out with a mattock. They passed a boat train, a whole string of boats selling watermelons, chickens and eggs, bananas, coffee, and sugarcane juice.

Intermingled with stretches of jungle were marshes and meadows. On islands in the river, David could see monkeys playing in the trees and flocks of bright parakeets. When the river wound through clammy hot miles of wild thick green foliage, he admired the orchids and the enormous butterflies; but he knew that underneath were the snakes and other creeping things. In the water, David saw giant catfish and huge electric eels and sometimes a crocodile, but most of these were gone. Always lots of mosquitoes waited to taste blood. Thus he proceeded to Manaus.

The state of Bahia on the northeast coast had kept much of the Portuguese and African influence of Brazil's past. After a Portuguese navigator had planted his flag there in 1500, Brazil remained a colony of Portugal for three centuries. Salvador, Bahia, once the capital of Brazil, was the spot where African slaves were sold at market for hundreds of years. Though the slaves had been freed in the nineteenth-century, African influences remained to rival the Portuguese cultural elements, and there were many black Baians.

The Portuguese had brought with them the Catholic religion and in Bahia had built cathedrals of splendor. As the slaves came ashore, they brought with them their African rituals of Candomble.

Thus spiritism mixed with Catholicism.

Along the railroad, Bahia Minas (which no longer exists), at Caravelas, David bought a house where he started a preaching point. Six months later, when the mission became a church, he was present for the organization service. The people were so happy about the church they kept him up talking until one o'clock in the morning. His train was to leave by 4:30 AM.

Though he never carried an alarm clock, David had not missed any trains or buses in the early mornings because the Lord always woke him up. That night at Caravelas, a little after one, he prayed, "Lord, will you please wake me at four so I can take that train?" Then he fell sound asleep.

All of a sudden he heard a noise. A cat was chasing a rat along the rafters of the house. Since the place was covered with tin, the animals bumping against it made loud reverberating sounds. He looked at his watch. It was four o'clock.

He rode the train as far as it went. If he missed his next plane connection, he would have to remain in Bahia for at least ten days.

Determined to go on, he stood by the roadside until a jeep came along packed with seven people. The driver stopped when he saw David waving, but there was no room for him on the inside of the vehicle. He picked up his bag and climbed with it onto the top of the jeep where he sat for four hours until his benefactors stopped and said, "We are going in another direction, so you had better get off. We are sorry there is no house nearby, but maybe someone else will come along."

He asked God to send some other transportation. This time the answer to his prayer was an oil truck. "I don't take passengers," the swarthy driver called out.

"But I'm not a passenger. I am a missionary."

"Very well. I will take you. But my truck doesn't have a starter. If the motor stops, it will just be too bad. This road is no good, so I know it will take at least ten hours to get to the next town. You dare to go?"

"I will go."

By nightfall, they arrived at a town and located a boarding-house. David's room looked fine, but he smelled a terrible odor.

When he opened the window, he quickly closed it. A drain pit outside made him shut the window to keep the fresh air in.

At the boardinghouse he met a Christian who asked, "Why don't you start Baptist work here?" He spoke that night to a small group of Christians and initiated a preaching point (which in a few months became a church). He felt that the Lord had put him in that spot at the right time.

Next morning another truck pulled the oil truck until it started. The driver said, "We have many hills to climb. If the motor goes dead, I don't know what we will do."

"Don't worry. We will arrive, and I will catch my plane."

They rolled downhill into a valley where the motor stopped.

"Now we have to stay here."

David prayed, "Oh, God, make the truck start." To the driver he said, "Try it again." When the motor cranked, the man said, "That's a miracle."

David answered, "The Lord put me by your side so you can know that he is the Lord of all."

(Ten years later David met this driver again and found out that he had been converted. The driver said he had never forgotten the first time he heard about Jesus beside David in an oil truck.)

They arrived at the air strip fifteen minutes before the plane was to leave. Because of that trip, a church had been planted and a truck driver won to Christ.

In 1954, Brazilian Baptists had work only in three places along the Sao Francisco River in the northeast. Consequently David made an effort to expand the Baptist witness there.

He boarded a river launch at Barra, a town surrounded by rugged desert country, and rode the ship upriver to Lapa, an eight-day trip.

While the river craft was refueling at Ibotirama, David talked with people near the dock. He saw a woman kneeling on a rocky ledge washing clothes in the river. In response to his questioning, the woman told him she was a Christian and would like to see Baptist work started in that town. As a result of the conversation, the Home Mission Board sent a missionary teacher there to start a school. Also a church and a Bible institute were established.

Lapa, David's destination, was built near a large rock, the site of several Catholic shrines, widely believed to be a place of miracles. Many priests and others went there once a year in August to burn candles and to worship.

The half a dozen Baptists in Lapa wanted a church but feared it would be impossible to have one in such a Catholic stronghold.

The boardinghouse where David stayed had a loudspeaker system which played records and announced news items, charging five cruzeiros for each announcement.

In Brazil all radio stations were required to stop their programs at 7 PM for an hour to give the government a chance to announce its news. A loudspeaker system had to follow the same rule. In the boardinghouse, David wrote a note: "A man arrived in Lapa this afternoon who is director of a radio Bible program in Rio de Janeiro. He will present a message this evening in the main square."

He handed this note to the loudspeaker announcer who objected, "The priest will oppose this."

David insisted: "Instead of five cruzeiros I will give you ten. The priest will not say anything."

Immediately the man broadcast the note. When he finished the priest, indeed, could not answer him on the loudspeaker because it was seven o'clock, and broadcasting had to stop for an hour.

In the meantime, the announcement brought a big crowd to the square to hear the visitor. When he started preaching, rocks spattered around him. Calmly he told the crowd, "Those rocks won't hurt me. I just want you to know that Jesus loves you, even though you sometimes don't have the assurance that he does." He talked with such kindness to the offenders that they stopped throwing rocks.

David started a school in Lapa. (Later the school building became a church. Some years afterward he spoke in the city; in two days fifty-two people accepted Jesus as Savior.)

In Central, Bahia, he established a medical clinic and organized a church. Because of the severe drought in Bahia, there was no running water and little drinking water available. David wanted very badly to take a bath, so the woman in whose home he was staying gave him a two-pound can of water. With that, he washed himself that night and saved enough to wash and shave himself the next morning.

From Central, David rode a truck out into the countryside and arranged for a ride back next day, but the driver forgot him. He had to walk twelve miles, carrying his suitcase. Finally he got a truck to Xique-Xique where he boarded a plane for Rio.

An attractive, young, red-haired missionary from Texas, Mary Ruth Carney, age twenty-eight, joined the Home Mission Board early in 1955, as personnel secretary. Three other associates were added to the Home Mission Board staff to assist David.

In early April, Mary Ruth left her office in Belo Horizonte to make a survey trip along the Tocantins River to carry money for missionary payrolls and to visit several schools, clinics, and an orphanage, to encourage the personnel, and to arrange for supplies.

In a commercial plane, she flew to Carolina, on the border of Goias and Maranhao, where Baptists had a primary shcool, high school, and Bible institute which trained workers for the interior.

At Carolina a range of mountains springs up between the Tocantins and the Araguaia, with flat tops and cliffed rims, but north of Carolina all is flatness to Belem.

Waldice Quieroz, one of the home missionaries at Carolina, and Mary Ruth contracted with a pilot to fly them to a remote orphanage at Itacaja. The plane that took the two from Carolina to Itacaja had to turn back with motor trouble.

At the orphanage, they distributed candy and spent several joyful hours playing with the children. Saturday, April 9, they planned to go on farther, to a clinic. Mary Ruth found another plane and pilot for hire. She was told that the pilot was good and the plane one of the finest.

A fifth passenger had been booked, though the plane was only certified for four. The plane took off and began to climb, but the motor missed. The pilot turned back toward the field. The motor got rougher, and the pilot banked again. As friends who had said good-bye stood below and watched, the plane fell to the ground and exploded in flames.

Very little could be found of the passengers. A stack of bills Mary Ruth had been taking to pay the missionaries had fallen from her suitcase. A letter to her parents was not burned. She was a Baptist minister's only child. Her parents had been eagerly awaiting her first furlough.

No telegram could be sent from Itacaja; however, David needed to establish identification before Mary Ruth's parents could be notified. A man on horseback rode as fast as he dared to the nearest commercial air strip. The news was wired to Rio. Missionaries telephoned David in Belo Horizonte where he was visiting his sisters. The once-a-week flight for Carolina happened to be leaving that day. From Carolina, he hired a small plane to Itacaja.

That day David presided over the burial of the ashes of Mary Ruth and Waldice. He said, "A blonde and a black, bound by the love of Jesus, died together to glorify God."

Reading his articles about the crash, many felt the call to enter into the missionary enterprise. Mary Ruth had been popular, especially among the young people. The Lord used her death to fire hearts; revivals came in many places as a result. Even a tragedy was turned into an opportunity to witness. Later a monument was erected at Itacaja, with the missionaries' names engraved in marble.

As David and his hired pilot were leaving Itacaja, he realized the frightening condition of the rough landing strip. It was so short and the trees at the end so tall that planes coming in to land had to come down. There would be no second chance. Takeoff was difficult, too, and that day David's pilot barely cleared the treetops.

When David flew a small plane to Rondonia to try to begin work among the Paacas Novos Indians, he entered an area very dangerous to fly in: rapid changes of weather, no air traffic control, and no weather service.

A missionary had been appointed to work with the Xerentes Indians in Mato Grosso and others to work with the Apinayes and the Paacas Novos.

As David arrived at a village of the Paacas Novos, he hung his hammock between two trees near the cluster of mud huts. The Indians wanted to sing for him, so he listened and then taught them some songs. They enjoyed this so much that several went to the woods, killed a monkey, and offered it to him for food.

He said, "I don't think I eat monkey, though I have never tried it." So they ate the monkey themselves. Again they went hunting, and this time they brought back a tapir.

"No," David said, "I don't eat that either."

On the next try, they brought a deer. He liked that, so he ate his fill and had some left over to supply him for several days on the road.

In this experience, David remembered how his mother had made him eat bitter gilo and told him he must learn to like anything God had given him for food.

This tribe of Indians were reported to be eaters of human flesh. However, David learned that they ate only the flesh of those who died naturally. The Home Mission Board was able to start a school taught by missionaries among these Indians. After a time of this Christian influence, the tribe gave up the custom of eating human flesh.

In the early 1960s, the Belem-Brasilia highway, the first major inland road to be constructed, cut a long, pink gash through the green of the endless forests. Before it was paved, rains would turn it to a red sea of mud. David began buying properties for the Home Mission Board near the highway so that eventually one hundred churches were organized along it.

While David was preaching at Alvorada City in 1965, the rains came. Buses stopped, and most people gave up trying to go anywhere. But David needed to go to Gurupy. When he saw a jeep parked at a crossroad, he waited beside it until the driver returned. At first, the man said he could not take riders. But David showed him his Bible and told him he was a missionary, so the driver allowed him to go along.

The way was exceedingly slippery, but suddenly a paved passage was revealed by the road side. The driver cut over toward it. David warned, "Maybe this is a private road. Perhaps you'd better not try it." But the driver went on anyway.

Near the end of the good road, as they were enjoying swift progress, appeared a fat man with a pistol in his hand. The driver stopped. The big fellow said, "Did you not know this is a private aeroplane landing strip? You get out, or I will shoot you."

The jeep driver got so nervous that David felt it was time to say something.

"I want to apologize for our intrusion. Just excuse him for driving on your road. I am a Baptist missionary, and I need to go to Gurupy today. You did not have your wind sock up, and we did not know your plane lands here. We will take the jeep away immediately. If you feel we ought to pay something, I think we can."

The man put away his gun. David left a Bible and some tracts. David and the driver returned to the dirt road. The driver stopped and wiped the perspiration off his brow. "I have a large family, and I thank you for saving my life."

David answered, "No, don't thank me. Thank God who sent me your way."

The man would not accept any pay for the trip.

Five or six days later, David met the man a second time. "You are here again?"

"Yes, I will be here for one more day or two. I shall never forget you. I will listen to the "Bible School of the Air" because I want to learn more about your faith in Jesus."

10

Family Time

I will pour my spirit upon thy seed, and my blessing upon thine off-spring: . . . One shall say, I am the Lord's; . . . and another shall sub-scribe with his hand unto the Lord (Isa. 44:3-5).

Soft music filtered through the house, mingling with other morning sounds of the city. The music awakened Ana Maria. She knew her father was home again, for that was the way he best liked to wake up his family. To know her father was there filled her with happiness. Since he had started traveling for the Home Mission Board, he was home maybe only ten days out of every thirty.

"Happy birthday, Sophia Regina!" David gave his third daughter a hug and a kiss on each cheek. She had been born January 21, 1955, a short time after his election to the Home Mission Board, and had been named for Sophia Nichols. A few minutes after she was born at one o'clock in the morning her dad had left for Porto Alegre on another missionary trip. "What shall we do today to celebrate?" he asked her.

"Let's go to the Park of the Emperor!" The family's favorite fun spot was in the Forest of Tijuca. They would drive up a mountain, past mansions almost hidden in the lush greenery, to the Capela Mayrinck at Bridal Veil Falls. The tiny chapel built in 1860 housed a painting by the famous artist, Portinari. But the spot that most attracted the Gomes children was an open space near the top of the waterfall; there they could picnic or play.

Two years after Sophia Regina, Esther Ruth had been born, on October 15, 1957. Then March 15, 1961, Elizabeth, the sixth child, arrived.

Five girls and one boy—Ana Maria, Priscila, Marcos, Sophia Regina, Esther Ruth, and Elizabeth—eagerly awaited family altar time each day. Each could decide, taking turns, what would be read and sung. Always David and Haydee had been willing to listen with open minds to other people's ideas. This courtesy they also accorded their children. All of them knew their own prayer requests were just as important as those of the grown-ups and would be considered with as much gravity.

The youngest ones could choose the form of worship the family altar time would follow. Today they sang choruses and marched around the room, as in Vacation Bible School. No matter what the form, though, this was a meaningful time to every family member.

When David had to be away for weeks or months, he could go in peace, knowing that Haydee would take care of the children, the family finances, the house, and any major problems of the Home Mission Board that might arise in his absence.

Both parents taught the children to study hard and try to do their best in everything. However, most of the child-rearing problems fell to Haydee because she was with the children more than her husband. (Later Sophia Regina remembered that "all punishment of us children was done with a great degree of love.")

All the children understood the reason for David's being away. They loved and respected him and, as a rule, did not insist on their own way.

Because David was often absent from home did not mean that he forgot his family. His interest in his children's gtowth—physical, mental, and spiritual—was real, and he found ways to show that he cared. His travels opened the world to them, through his letters, cards, and the gifts he never failed to bring. These gifts usually carried some meaning or message, which he could use as an object lesson to teach his youngsters to love people in other states and lands, no matter who the people were or what they looked like.

David's brief times at home were full of joy, devotional moments, sight-seeings, visiting, and entertaining friends. No decision of importance was made at his house without his seeking God's leadership in it through Bible reading and prayer. Always on his visits home, the first and last thing he did was to gather his wife and children together and praise God for his goodness.

All of his children could see the love of their parents for each other and knew that their faith was one of works, as well as one of words.

In his quest to make Christ known, David did not neglect witnessing to his own children. All of them became Christians in early childhood.

11

All on the Altar

Present your bodies a living sacrifice, holy, acceptable unto God, which is your reasonable service (Rom. 12:1).

Was it the clang of a tram that awakened him? Or the noise of fireworks in somebody's midnight celebration? David opened his eyes, still half-asleep. Where was he? Oh, yes. Back home in Rio.

He heard footsteps and the sound of someone coughing. From the bedroom doorway, he could see into the kitchen. Their missionary guest was not drinking water in the glass provided for her, but from one of the family glasses.

Quickly he tiptoed back to bed. For a long time, he lay wondering what to do. She had been one of the first missionaries sent out by the Home Mission Board and had started the work in north Goias out near the Amazon. Brazilian Baptists loved and respected her. How could he embarrass her, perhaps hurt her feelings? Yet he must think of his family.

Next morning he and Haydee talked with her.

"Have you been drinking from our glasses all week?" Haydee asked.

The missionary admitted she had. "I didn't see any need to have a separate glass."

"Remember, I asked you to promise to do that when I brought you here," David reminded her. "We must think of the children."

"But I don't have anything contagious."

"Today we will take you to a doctor so that he can examine you. Maybe he can give you something to help your cough."

After the doctor had X-rayed the missionary, he talked privately with David. "She cannot live long for her tuberculosis is far advanced."

The X rays of the Gomes family showed no trace of disease, but the doctor told them it might show up fifteen days after a person had been exposed. "If any one of you has a swelling of the throat, that could be the beginning," he warned.

David spent the next twenty days traveling in north Brazil, with little rest. When he got home, only Sophia Regina was there with a servant. She told him, "Daddy, my neck hurts." The knot on her neck looked like a swollen gland.

Another X ray of the child showed the disease had not yet entered her lungs, but was in the throat. The doctor predicted that with medicine he was prescribing she should be all right soon.

On the same day, however, David's X-ray revealed tuberculosis in the upper part of both lungs. Sent to bed for a month, David soon grew restless and unhappy. Yet Haydee remained optimistic and often found reasons to say, "David, let's praise God. He is good."

At the end of the fourth week, David was much better. Against doctor's orders, he planned a long trip. "I'll take all the precautions I can," David stubbornly insisted. He rode a horse to a river where he baptized a group of new Christians. As he started to mount his horse to leave, he suddenly felt nauseated and weak and leaned his head against the animal. "Something is wrong," he told the others. He canceled the rest of the trip and flew home.

Now the doctor told him, "You are worse than you were in the beginning. Much worse."

To get away from the oppressing heat of Rio, David took his family to Curitiba, to the home of Haydee's father.

Often David had a slight fever and pain in his chest. Many nights he could not sleep. A nurse came to the house periodically to give him injections. One morning she said, "I can't find a vein I have not already stuck with a needle!"

"I'm sorry," he answered, "but I don't have anything to do with my veins!" He couldn't understand why the medicine was not helping, why he was not getting better. Though he laughed with the nurse, he felt terrible.

An associational meeting was scheduled near Londrina. Since it was accessible by plane, Haydee agreed that David might attempt it.

In Londrina, seeking a place where he could be alone, David entered the First Baptist Church and sat down in the quietness to talk with God.

Outside the church, noise and reddish-purple dust saturated the atmosphere. Farmers had come to the city to buy or sell coffee, their shoes muddy with red dirt. Beyond the tall buildings were the warehouses, and out on the edge of the city curving rows of coffee trees reached farther than the eye could see.

From his quiet spot in the sanctuary, David could not hear the honking of the taxi cabs or the shouting of the traders. He realized there must be some lessons God was teaching him through his illness. As he sat praying, he did not ask God to heal him; he looked up and thanked God for his presence with him and for his love and mercy.

He leafed through a hymnal to one of his favorites: "His constant presence beside me/Strengthens my feeble heart/Keeps me and helps me in trials/Drives away my doubt."

He opened his Bible and read some passages that he had underlined. One was 1 Corinthians 2:9-10: "Eye hath not seen, nor ear heard, neither have entered into the heart of man, the things which God hath prepared for them that love him. But God hath revealed them unto us by his Spirit: for the Spirit searcheth all things, yea, the deep things of God."

Another was in John 15:7: "If ye abide in me, and my words abide in you, ye shall ask what ye will, and it shall be done."

This thought came: *What shall I do? I'll just lay my life on the altar and leave it there. That's what Paul meant when he said, "I beseech you, therefore, by the mercies of God, that you present your bodies a living sacrifice, wholly acceptable to God." I lay it all on the altar. My body is there, my mind, my heart, my feet, my will, my money. My today is there, my tomorrow, my future. Everything is on the altar.*

As David prayed, there came the feeling that two big hands took hold of his back and pressed down gently on his lungs, taking away his disease. He felt new strength flow into him.

This occurred during his second year as secretary of the Home

Mission Board. From that day, David started traveling more than ever before; the symptoms of tuberculosis never returned.

"I know that it was the healing touch of Jesus on my back," he wrote in his journal.

Church of Hope's first regular meeting place in Rio. Vacant lot behind the fence is the site of the Building of Faith.

David Gomes, speaking, is shown with Jimmy Allen, then president of the Southern Baptist Convention. Allen spoke during the cornerstone laying ceremony on August 27, 1978.

Choirs from Higienopolis Church and Church of Hope sang at the cornerstone laying ceremony.

Bible reading marathon at the Church of Hope

Young people make a chain of prayer down the mountainside at Camp Mount Moriah.

David Gomes baptizing new Christians in a stream near Passa Quarto

David Gomes, Anne Washburn McWilliams, and Jose Luis Martinez on November 21, 1980, at the 75th anniversary of the Baptist Spanish Publishing House, El Paso, Texas. Martinez translated *David Gomes: When Faith Triumphs* into Spanish.

12

"Go Find My Sheep"

What man of you, having a hundred sheep, if he lose one of them, doth not leave the ninety and nine in the wilderness, and go after that which is lost, until he find it? (Luke 15:4).

The reddening sky at daybreak changed the silken waters of the Araguaia River into a path of fire before the oncoming river-boat. David sang his favorite hymn as he set up his portable type-writer on a box at knee level.

> Lord, I would clasp thy hand in mine,
> Nor ever murmur nor repine,
> Content, whatever lot I see,
> Since 'tis thy hand that leadeth me!

On these long river trips, he kept describing the scenes as he saw them. Ever since he had become executive secretary of the Home Mission Board, he had written an article a week for *O Jornal Batista*. Always, too, he found plenty of material in his journal for the home missions magazine he edited.

In the thin mist of morning, a fish leapt out of the water and fell back with a splash. A hummingbird hovered over the boat and soon was gone in the half-mile trip across the river. In the white sand alongside the stream, David had seen tracks of a deer, iguanas, and turtles, and at one place the tracks of a jaguar. Birds were every-where—toucans, parrots, wild ducks, and pigeons. Now he heard the tapping of a woodpecker.

Palm trees and thick greenery edged the sand. Beyond that on the east was desert scrub. To the west, was jungle. Frequently the boat passed huge golden sand banks in the strong, but slow, flow-ing river.

The Araguaia is a beautiful river, David thought. *Its clear waters are a contrast to the Tocantins that has muddy water like the Mississippi. Yet the Araguaia is often a river of upheaval, and the Tocantins is a safe river.*

Sometimes David felt that he could compare Araguaia with the sea that pretended to be nice, yet could hurt and kill men. Was this not true in life? Often what appeared beautiful turned out to be full of danger.

Small boats themselves he had found to be a missionary field. The crewmen, the passengers, citizens he met when the boat docked—he saw all as individuals for whom Jesus cared. At all hours, he never forgot his desire to tell people about Jesus.

One night on the Tocantins, the riverboat captain had announced, "We can't go any further because the rudder is broken."

While waiting for the repairs, David flashed a light along the banks and saw light in the window of a small house on a hill. He walked up to the door and knocked.

"The doctor has arrived!" the man of the house called excitedly. His wife was ill, and he had sent for a doctor.

"No, I am not a doctor. I am a missionary. I preach Jesus. He can help your wife get well." David prayed for the woman. He gathered leaves from an orange tree to make a tea to calm her nerves. Also he found some aspirin in his bag and gave her a couple. Soon she said she felt much better.

As he was leaving, he told her, "I want you to know that Jesus loves you and wants you to love him."

When he got back to the boat, the repairs had been completed. He felt that God had stopped the boat so he could witness to that family at a time when they needed help.

As the riverboat passed a small village on a bluff above the stream, he heard a dog barking. This reminded him of the funny incident that had happened at Araguacema.

He had already gone to sleep at the boardinghouse when something cold touched his back. He jumped up in alarm. But it was only a dog licking his back through a hole in the hammock.

So many funny incidents happened in his travels, he had started writing a humor column for the home mission magazine. He called it *O Sertao Pitoresco* (The Funny Hinterland):

The old man came after me before dark. I did not expect to be called in the dark, but he explained: "When the rooster crows, I have my feet in the world." That rooster positively was not my friend.

We visited a home, the place where the priest was usually entertained. The lady said immediately: "I do not want *culto* (worship) here. I am Catholic and do not admit *culto* in my house." We decided to stay a little longer. As we talked, the woman said, "I have decided to allow you to sing your songs, make your prayers, and read your Bible, but worship—this, no!"

In a little village in Pernambuco, men talked about the sugarcane plantation: 'If the rain comes happy, we shall have a lot of sugar cane this year.'

He turned to his typewriter. He had decided which story to use in *A Patria Para Cristo:*

It was near noon in the jungle when Manoel and I left on horseback. Since there would be no possibility of our finding food along the way, we took our own lunch. I had a can packed with chicken and other food. I had seven bananas and some chocolate bars. Chocolate I always took with me when I planned to visit missionaries who worked in small villages where they could not buy it.

As we came down the mountain, we stopped to tour a factory that made raincoats. The workers used a milk-like gum to cover the material to make it resistant to rain.

Then we rode until around 6:30. It started getting dark, so I asked my friend, "Manoel, can we sleep here? We could hang our hammocks on a tree. My back is getting sore, and it's hurting."

He looked at me and said, "If you are afraid of jaguars, we had better go on."

My pains just went away, and we kept going! By seven we arrived at a little hut beside the trail. It had a porch where we could hang our hammocks and spend the night without bothering the people inside. The woman of the house said we could stay there.

I inquired about taking a bath. The woman said, "You shouldn't go to the river here because some wild beast might hurt you. You'd better not try." Anyhow, I felt I couldn't do without a bath. We decided to go on and risk the animals, but nothing happened.

We were tying our hammocks when six children came in. They looked so hungry that I gave each one a banana, and I had one left.

Though we hadn't noticed him at first, a drunkard was sitting in a corner of the porch. Now he started singing a song, "Softly and Tenderly Jesus Is Calling."

I asked him, "Do you know that hymn?"

He said, "I have been in churches where they sing this, and I think it is pretty."

I asked, "Why do you get so drunk if you believe in Jesus?"

He said, "Because I don't need him." After a little while he asked, "Why are you here? Did you come to bring peace or did you come to bring war?"

I answered, "I am a missionary of God, and I bring peace, so I want to give you this banana. Will you please go and eat it outside?" The man left.

Manoel looked at me and said, "Do you know where I saw him the last time? It was in the Dianopolis Saloon. This man is not a desirable character." I soon wished that Manoel had not said that because the drunkard heard him and came back in.

He drew his dagger and pointed to Manoel: "Look at this man! I am going to cut him in little pieces."

When he said that, the children and the woman of the house came to see what was happening. I turned to the man and said, "I am a missionary, and I am here to bring the peace of God. The man of this house is not at home. Will you please keep quiet?"

He said, "If he doesn't apologize, I am going to cut him up completely!"

I said to Manoel, "Will you apologize to him?"

"I thought I told the truth."

"You forget that and apologize."

Manoel asked him to forgive him, and the man said, "If it were not for the missionary, you would be in little pieces by this time." Then he went out and yelled until midnight, and we could not sleep. We asked the woman if she had something to eat.

She said, "The little I have I must keep. When my husband returns I will need food for him, so there is nothing I can give you."

I called Manoel and said, "Let's eat some of the food we have in that can because there is nothing else, but let's save the most we can. We still have one day of the trip and likely won't find any food tomorrow." We ate about half the food and kept the other half for next day. Then we went to our hammock and tried again to sleep, but of course could not. About two o'clock we got up to feed and water the horses so we could leave at five. We needed to reach the next town before nightfall.

At two, I found the dark-haired little woman, the owner of the house, already beating her cotton. She had a rather nice table with the cotton spread over it. With a rod, she would beat it and beat it until it became shaggy. Later she would put it in a treadle machine and make thread and then weave that into cloth.

I asked, "Do you have some tea or coffee?"

She said, "There is no sugar and no coffee. I could make tea from orange leaves, but I wouldn't have sugar for it."

"Well, just give me some hot water."

She boiled the water, and I took the chocolate bars I had brought for the missionaries. I put them in the boiling water and we had hot chocolate. She said, "I never tasted anything like that in my life!"

As we drank together, I said, "I want you to know I really am a missionary. Last night we could not read the Bible on account of the drunkard, but I want to read for you a story that Jesus told." I read the 15th chapter of Luke, the whole chapter.

She said, "I want to be a Christian. There is no church near here, though, and no preacher. I was amazed last night at the way you treated that drunkard. This man has been a problem to us, and I hope some day he will go somewhere else."

We prayed together. Then Manoel and I saddled the horses and left. We rode next morning on horseback until 10 o'clock and when we saw a big truck coming our way, we stopped the driver and asked if we might ride with him to the next town. He said, "I can take you, but I can't take the horses." We left the horses with two men who said they would take care of them until Manoel could come back and get them two days later.

The truck was loaded with rice, covered with sailcloth for protection against rain. We got under the sailcloth.

Underneath, I heard somebody chewing and I asked, "Is somebody eating here?" A voice answered, "Yes, this is an old woman eating a piece of meat."

"Will you give me a piece? I'm hungry."

"I will if you will give me something in return."

I promised that at the next stop I would pay her, so she gave me a little piece of dried meat. We ate, Manoel and I, and, it was good for us.

An hour or two later, the truck stopped to let us out. When we turned the sailcloth back I could see that the old woman had white hair and not a single tooth. I gave her some money. There were some oranges at the place where we stopped, so I bought some for her. She was happy that she had helped us.

At the end of the day, we arrived in the little town where I was to preach.

Since there were no banks in most of the villages where the home missionaries were, the question of how to get money to them was an ever-recurring one. Almost always, when possible, David delivered the money himself. He would wrap it in newspaper, place it in a briefcase, and cover the package with tracks and leaflets. As he traveled he could continually open the briefcase, giving tracts to one person and then to another.

When he stopped to spend the night, he would hold up the briefcase and say to the people at the boardinghouse, "This is my pillow." He felt sure that this way nobody would take the money.

One night in Bahia he had a lot of money. At Xique-Xique on the Sao Francisco River, he preached in an evangelistic service, and four men were converted. Late that night, he entered a boardinghouse.

At least fifteen men were sleeping in the same room. This time he was uneasy about the money and felt that God was directing him to take it to someone else's house.

He wrapped the briefcase in a newspaper and took it to the home of one of the men who had accepted Jesus that night. The man promised to keep the package for him until the next day.

About two o'clock in the morning he woke up and saw somebody walking toward him. He sat up on his mattress (all were sleeping on mattresses on the floor), and said, "What is it, friend? Are you sick? Do you need something?"

The man answered, "No, I am not sick."

David had spent the rest of the night watching from his vantage point on the floor, but nothing else happened.

Returning from his reverie, he realized that now it was midmorning on the riverboat, and he was thirsty. One of the boatmen gave him a coconut. He cut a hole in it and drank the milk, a drink as refreshing as water.

On one trip, he recalled, he had been so thirsty he feared collapse. To catch a plane around 4:30 in the afternoon, he had to walk a mile in hot sunlight from the little city to the air field. His throat was parched, and he felt dizzy. Friends with him pointed to a small unclean stream, but he told them, "I won't drink that water."

"Then you are not thirsty."

"If I drink this water, I would be sick. I'd rather die thirsty and in good health than to drink this water and be sick!"

They were amazed that he wouldn't drink the water even though he was so thirsty. At the airport, he waited until the small plane came. Inside the plane he had a cool drink of water.

Now he looked at the clear water of the Araguaia. A gull lightly skimmed the river with its beak, drinking as it flew. *How important water is,* he thought. And the longing consumed him to share the Water of life with all of Brazil.

He leafed through his journal and found an entry made while traveling with Elton Johnson, a missionary in North Brazil at Corrente:

We were in a jeep and the radiator was leaking. We had to travel the whole night in a tremendous section of Piaui where the jaguars are many. We had to stop often because the jeep would get hot and we would have to put water in it. A hot dry wind was blowing off the desert. We crossed steep gullies and dry river beds. Some places where we stopped to get water were just stagnant pools.

"Don't fall in," Dr. Johnson warned me. "The piranhas might eat you!" Finally he said, "This is the last stop we are going to make tonight because there is no more water along the rest of the way."

I prayed, "Oh, God, I want you to help us to find what is wrong with this jeep. We need to get to the other place and we just can't spend the night stranded on the road."

The Lord answered my prayer. I told Dr. Johnson, "Look at that radiator once more. Maybe there is something we can repair." There at the last source of water, he found that the drain plug was open. We tightened it, and the water didn't leak out any more.

When possible David traveled by small plane. One trip he would never forget, for lightning struck the plane. The plane flipped over and left him hanging upside down by his seat belt. The pilot, who had said he did not believe in Jesus, screamed, "Pray for us, or we are going to die!"

David reassured him, "The Lord will help us. We are not going to die."

They landed safely.

On one occasion, David had located a place from the air

where he thought he should go down and try to organize a church. From Porto Nacional, his plane for some reason changed its route, so he flew over territory he had not seen before. From the air, he could see two small towns connected by a bridge. When the plane stopped in Dianopolis, Goias, he asked the missionary, Clovis Lopes de Zouza, the name of those towns and about a way to get there.

Next morning he left on horseback. After he crossed two small rivers and climbed a mountain he arrived at Rio da Conceicao at 4 PM.

He found a boardinghouse where he could spend the night and was directed to the river as the place to take a bath. The middle-aged landlady wore a red flowered dress and sandals. Her hair was pulled into a knot on the back of her head.

She said, "Before entering the bathing spot, you ask 'Is anybody there?' If some women answer, you must wait until they finish."

In Rio da Conceicao, David preached in the square and drew a crowd. Those converted formed the nucleus for a church later.

Experiences like these David could remember by the dozens. For the most part, these are happy. He began to sing again, "Content, whatever lot I see, for 'tis thine hand that leadeth me."

At noon, the riverboat landed at his destination. David then took a plane back to Porto Nacional in north Goias and on to Rio.

13

The Church of Hope

Fear not, little flock; for it is your Father's good pleasure to give you the kingdom (Luke 12:32).

During almost a century of Baptist work in Brazil, downtown Rio de Janiero remained without a single Baptist church. Though David longed to witness to the thousands who come and go there, he had not thought of organizing a downtown church. Then one event led to another, like a row of dominoes falling, in such a way that he could not doubt God's leadership.

While David was in Lapa, Bahia, on business for the Home Mission Board, the rains came strong and sudden. No one could travel. Planes canceled flights. Roads turned to slippery mire. Overcrowded river boats could not squeeze in even one more passenger, so David stayed in Lapa for a week.

As he listened to his own radio program each day, he felt an urge to buy a headquarters site for the "Bible School of the Air."

He laid out a plan he called the "S Operation" for *sede*—headquarters in Portuguese. Uually it was difficult for him to keep a secret. Yet his own family did not know what the "S Operation" was.

At length, back in Rio, he launched a series of radio announcements: "The S is coming. We want one thousand to give five thousand cruzeiros and five thousand to give one thousand cruzeiros for the 'S Operation.' " For the first time, he asked directly for money for the radio program. Always before he had felt his responsibility was to concentrate entirely on the Home Mission Board offerings, but he was beginning to realize the importance of radio in communicating the gospel message.

When David finally told the secret, listeners sent offerings, but not enough to buy a house or apartment anywhere near the downtown where he hoped the headquarters could be. In the meantime, he deposited the money in a special "*SEDE*" account to draw interest.

One afternoon a woman came to see him. She said, "Pastor, I have been a listener of the "Bible School of the Air" since the beginning. I have given my money through the years to help support it. When you started the 'S Operation' I was one of the one thousand who sent five thousand cruzeiros. Now you never mention it. What happened to our gifts?"

He looked at the woman, white hair and dark brown eyes, three times a widow, in her sixties, and said, "I accept the rebuke. You are right. The money could not buy the house we needed, so for the time being it is in the bank."

"Then you should tell that to your listeners." She adjusted her crocheted shawl.

"No. Here is today's paper. Let's look at it and see what we can do with the money." They prayed and asked God to show them a place for the headquarters.

Real estate ads that day listed one apartment that could be bought with the amount of money in hand. It was fifty meters square (1 meter equals 39.37 inches). The owner, a Frenchman, had throat cancer and planned to return to France.

After David bought the place, he tried to make maximum use of it. The apartment had one large room plus a bathroom and a small entrance hall. A miniature soundproof recording studio was added, plus built-in bookshelves, desk, and a few chairs.

With Home Mission Board duties continuing, David rarely had time to go to the apartment. But he announced that the headquarters had been bought and that visitors might stop by to see it or meet there for a prayer service once a week.

The little room was packed for the first prayer service. As the group expanded, the meetings moved to the local YMCA. On May 1, 1965, however, they moved back to the apartment. Only four were present. That night David directed the meeting and preached on "The God of Little Things," from Luke 12:32 "Fear not, little flock; for it is your Father's good pleasure to give you the kingdom."

He said, "I took my family and a friend to the zoological gardens. After we got home I asked the children, 'What did you like best in the zoo?' Our friend said, 'I liked the lions and the elephants and the rhinoceros.' I realized she liked everything big. I turned to my six-year-old boy to find out his impressions. 'Daddy, what I liked best was the little bird in a cage.'

"The same God who made the big elephants, the lions, the tigers, made the little bird, the pretty little bird. He made the big things, and he made the small things."

As the little group continued to meet, David began thinking of organizing a church in the downtown area. It was a long way from people's homes, but surely there must be a way to minister to those who were in town during the week. Yet the only available meeting place seemed impossibly small.

The reasons a church had not previously been started in the area were still valid. Real estate prices were enormous. Few Baptists lived in the area. It might be a task to get people together whose homes were scattered everywhere else in the city. Too, David still stayed busy with responsibilities for the Home Mission Board.

As he looked for a possible church meeting house, the apartment next door to the headquarters went on sale. David considered buying it and tearing down the wall between the two, but the owner's original price was too high.

A meeting place on ground level with an entrance from the street would be better. David doubted if the people he hoped to reach would venture into a building and ride elevators up to the tenth floor.

He looked at seven other places. At one of them he heard a man say, "No Protestant will get this place," so he stopped bidding, as he didn't want to quarrel.

Shortly after that the real estate agent called and said, "Pastor, I was impressed when you gave up the deal to that group opposing you. I promise that any time a good property is to be sold in town, I'll call you first."

While David was on a business trip to Sao Paulo on March 31, 1964, a revolution broke out, so he went back to Rio right away.

He found a note: "I have a house for you—Domingos."

The two drove to 127 First of March Street where they found an old house built by slaves, according to the deed, in 1752.

The old house, full of lumber and building materials, captured David's imagination. Its price was fifty-five thousand dollars or one hundred thousand cruzeiros. It was in front of the General Navy Administration Building and a navy hospital, on one of the most heavily traveled streets in the city. Sailors worked at the docks a few blocks away. The Bank of Brazil had headquarters on the same street. Other nearby buildings housed lawyers' offices and banks. Within sight was the Catholic cathedral, Candelaria, where the city's most fashionable weddings occurred.

Only twelve people were regularly attending the weekly prayer meetings at the apartment, but David envisioned many more being reached. He saw the area as a tremendous opportunity for home missions ministries. Some agreed with him but didn't think the money for a church building would ever be obtained.

Since David knew real estate prices would be more likely to rise than to fall, he concluded it was a time for boldness. He wanted to do as he felt God wanted him to do, though it seemed too difficult. So confident was he of God's leading in this purchase that he called the owner and told him, "We will buy it."

Next day David met the lawyer to draw up the papers. He phoned the Baptist Loan Board to ask for a promised loan but was told the money was not available at that time.

David turned pale.

"You don't have the down payment?" the owner guessed.

"No."

"How much do you have?"

"Ten thousand cruzeiros." (The Bible School of the Air had already designated this much for the cause.)

"We can set up the document for that, and I can wait twenty days for the other twenty thousand."

Instantly David felt God would approve of this arrangement, so he said, "I'll do it."

At home he made a list of persons he thought could help with loans or gifts. Next day he was leaving on a twenty day trip to

Amazonia and the territories. He left the list with Haydee, trusting the business to her and God.

When he spoke that night, twenty people accepted Jesus as Savior and twenty more answered the call to mission service. Ann Wollerman, a Southern Baptist missionary, gave him a contribution to the building.

He flew to Manaus, the fabled rubber boom city in the jungle, a thousand miles from the sea. Its opera house had once rivaled those in Europe. From the plane, he could see the spot where the dark waters of the Rio Negro joined the yellow waters of an Amazon tributary. Moist cobbled streets and the waterfront marketplace swarmed with people. On rooftops, clouds of *urubus*, or vultures, roosted.

The city was an ideal place to make an excursion into the Amazonian jungle; to visit Indian villages; to see great jungle orchids; or marvel at colorful macaws, noisy monkeys, and brilliant butterflies. But David planned to spend his time in Manaus visiting the missionaries, Lonnie Doyle and Loyd Moon. He asked them if it would be possible to contact Haydee, but Moon suggested he wait until he reached Belem. "If you sent a telegram here, it would take twenty days to reach Rio."

In the territory of Rondonia, David organized a mission. He traveled back to Manaus, on to Santarem by riverboat, and from there to Belem by plane.

"The city of mango trees," Belem is called. On the Para River, which borders the delta of the Amazon on the south and east, it is a miniature glimpse of the vast Amazon Valley. Just below the equator, its public park is a chunk of jungle. This was the city where the Baptist missionary, Erik Nelson, had arrived in 1891.

When David arrived in the city, he had a tremendous disappointment. There was no news from home; he wanted to know how things were there.

At his hotel, he got a call from the airline asking if he still planned to fly north. They wanted his answer within twenty minutes. Several other travelers were waiting on standby.

David knelt and asked the Lord what to do—go north or back

south to Rio. He said, "Lord, give me an answer through your Word."

When he opened the Bible, he saw that the pages had fallen to Psalm 21. Beside verses 2, 3, and 4, he wrote: "Belem, April 20, 1966," for God in those verses had given him a promise which was the desire of his heart.

Immediately, he called the airline and told them he was going north. The same night, Haydee called everyone on the list who had promised to lend or give money to buy the building for the church. Several on this list could not honor their promises. However, when she came to the end of the list, she had what she needed to make the down payment, plus the bus fare downtown to sign the documents and close the sale.

June 6, 1966, the first prayer service was held in the building at 127 First of March Street, while the rooms were still full of junk and before the lodger moved. As customary, lodgers charged for moving out. This one wanted eight thousand cruzeiros but permitted a prayer service in his home before he left.

Seven men prayed together, sang a hymn, and started cleaning the dirtiest place they had seen in a long time. While they were working, David walked across the street to the navy hospital to witness to the patients. One sailor who that afternoon accepted Christ died the next day.

On August 14, 1966, the Church of Hope was constituted. David had issued an invitation on the radio for the public to attend the organizational meeting. Such a large crowd arrived that they spilled over into the second floor of the building and out to the front sidewalk and into the street, causing a traffic jam. The general secretary of Baptists of the state presided. Visiting pastors represented several sections of the country.

Of all who came to see, only nineteen stood to say, "We will be members of the Church of Hope." Of the nineteen, one moved the next day to another city. In the beginning, the outlook was bleak. Yet David did not have a doubt that this was a project that God would bless.

14

The Kaleidoscope

All things work together for good to them that love God, to them who are the called according to his purpose (Rom. 8:28).

"Salvation results from our encounter with a Person. The touch of our faith in the heart of Jesus brings liberty and life. It is to be partakers in his nature, and not only imitators of his virtues."

Miami, 1965, at the Baptist World Alliance, David spoke on "Salvation and the Savior." Before he had finished, the buzzer sounded. The pastors called, "Let him continue! Let him continue!" Afterward many rushed forward to embrace him.

Over the hubbub, David heard a question, "Would you like to go to Australia to deliver this message?" It was the voice of Ray Taylor, representative of Baptists from Down Under. The invitation, accepted two years later, turned out to be a pivotal point in David's ministry.

Emotional turmoil had filled David's week in Miami, for he could not forget his troubles of preceding months. Criticism of his work had arisen. This time the barbs had cut deep. He had not been able to shake them off, as he customarily did.

His sympathetic leadership had won friends for him all over Brazil. But, as with most leaders, people eventually began to find fault. Some of the criticisms were merited. Others were not.

In a conference of Baptist leaders, held in Fortaleza, a pastor raised a question: "We need to find out where Pastor David Gomes spends all the money he receives. The Home Mission Board gets more than any Baptist agency in Brazil. What is he doing with it?"

One of David's associates, who was at the meeting, recorded the long discussion about money and took the tape back home to David.

"What's on it?"

"What they said about you."

"Throw it in the wastebasket. I don't want to hear it. I have read in the Bible a verse that says, 'Give no place to evil.' "

David had continually set higher and higher offering goals before Brazilian Baptists for the work of home missions. In his numerous trips to the interior, he had established new schools and medical clinics and organized new churches. For these, and for sites of future churches and institutions, he bought properties all over the country. He foresaw—accurately, as it turned out—that as roads were built and civilization moved westward, the population would increase and land prices would rise. He wanted to buy land for future use before the cost got any higher.

In Imperatriz, Maranhao, on the Trans-Amazon Highway, David bought a whole block of land. Its strategic location later made it an ideal place for the relocation of a Bible institute.

As times changed, the government opened more schools, and home missions methods and emphases changed. The number of Baptist schools was reduced. Because of this, some property that David had bought was sold, but at a higher price than the original purchase price. Other properties were used for new church sites, as he had planned.

Because David worked day and night, without vacation or rest, he expected the same of the missionaries working with him under Home Board appointment. Though he had the ability to express God's impression to him, in speaking and in fluent writing, he could also be impatient and impulsive. If his fellow workers did not catch the vision he felt they should, he would talk roughly to them.

His own dreams and ideals were so far above the average person's and he could see the end result so plainly that he could not understand how others could fail to grasp the vision too.

The missionaries were dedicated, hardworking, but they were tired. Many of them did not have the endless energy with which David had been endowed. Some felt too much was being asked of them. Possibly this started the winds of criticism blowing.

Then came plans for a nationwide campaign of evangelism. Until that time the Department of Evangelism had been a part of the Home Mission Board. Because of the growth of home mission work and the extensiveness of the planned campaign, many felt that a separate Board of Evangelism should be organized. Articles began to appear in the Baptist newspaper in support of this.

David disagreed. He answered these articles in the paper. He thought of evangelism as an area of home missions and felt it would be confusing to have another Board of Evangelism. Though the creation of a new board was not intended as a criticism or threat to the work of the existing Board, David viewed it that way.

Finally the decision about the new board was to be made during a convention at Belo Horizonte, David's home city.

The week before the convention, David had floated in a canoe down the Tocantins and hiked through the forest to the mission farm which grew rice and beans and raised cattle for the dining rooms of two orphanages, two Bible institutes, and a couple of medical centers. His sermon at the farm resulted in professions of faith.

He left about six in the evening. Since going upriver would take three times as long as going downriver, he figured it would be morning before he reached his destination.

With leaves he plucked from an overhanging tree, David made a pillow and soon fell asleep. About three o'clock in the morning, the other two men started yelling. The canoe had struck a rock in the river. David got up to help maneuver the craft over a difficult place; they managed to free it without overturning. He thanked God for the deliverance and went back to sleep. It was daylight when he awoke.

When he got to the convention in Belo, it was intermission time. Unnoticed, he entered a circle of men talking in the church vestibule. The men were laughing and enjoying each other's company.

One said, "We've got to stop this man [he had not seen David standing there]. How can a board grow like this Home Mission Board? How can we imagine the tail bigger than the dog?" All of them laughed; David slipped away and entered the auditorium.

After much discussion, those present voted by written ballot, yes or no, concerning the organization of a new Board of Evangelism. The votes for the new board won over the proposition to stay with the Home Mission Board by about twenty votes.

Another intermission followed. While David was outside, the man who had been presiding walked over to him and said, "David, I know the difference was close. Maybe you can find someone who voted in favor who is ready to ask for a reconsideration. The margin was so tight perhaps we should think about this more carefully."

"No, I don't fight conventions. I accept the decision of the majority. When I arrive in Rio next Monday, I'll be ready to turn everything over to the new Board of Evangelism."

Nevertheless, he left the convention with a sore heart and went to his room at the hotel. He thought, *If God could deliver me over a rock in the river, he can deliver me over this hard place too.*

He knelt and prayed, "Oh, God, if you are really with me still in my ministry, I want tonight when I preach to have at least twenty young people make their surrender to the missionary cause."

Though he felt hurt, he returned to the night session. When he preached and gave the invitation, thirty came forward, many accepting Jesus as Savior.

Once he had preached a sermon on Romans 8:28 and called it "The Kaleidoscope." His life had been like that kaleidoscope, with good parts and bad parts continually falling into the picture. He knew that God could use the bad parts to teach him some lesson or for some purpose known only to God. He could combine the bright parts and the dark ones to create an exquisite design.

That same night the aged pastor Florentino Ferreira told David that his mother had dedicated him to the Lord before his birth. Franquelina had never told David, and he had never known it until then.

15

Decision in Australia

He hath put a new song in my mouth (Ps. 40:3).

A Sunday afternoon in Sao Paulo, 1964, a rally took place in Roosevelt Square, an open area downtown as big as ten city blocks. Thirty thousand people jammed into the upper half of the square.

Earl Peacock, a Southern Baptist missionary, touched his young son's arm and said, "Son, look up because you will never see anything like this again."

Peacock had invited David to be the speaker for this closing rally of an evangelism campaign, to present Christ as the only hope to the millions in Sao Paulo. More had heard the gospel in Sao Paulo that week than at any time in the city's history. Similar campaigns had been going on all across Brazil.

People who came forward at the close of David's message brought the number of decisions in the open-air meetings that week to five hundred; another three thousand had registered decisions in revival meetings in the city churches.

At sundown, the meeting in Roosevelt Square ended. A parade formed to march a mile and a half from the square to Praca da Se where the crusade would officially close.

First in the parade were flags, then girls dressed in white to represent the churches, then came a float with a large Bible. Pastors, evangelists, the choir, the band, a hundred boys carrying posters, *Cristo a Unica Esperanca* (Christ the Only Hope) were followed by the thirty thousand people at the rally. Five thousand others joined the parade along the way.

Accompanied by the band, the paraders sang hymns. Instead of images and lighted candles, customary in religious parades, these marchers held their Bibles high.

The Praca da Se was changed to a gigantic cathedral under the

114

sky. Rubens Lopes, Sao Paulo pastor and director of the Sao Paulo crusade, told the crowd that Baptist churches attack no religion but simply preach Christ as Savior.

It was the following July, while in Miami, that David received the invitation to Australia mentioned in the previous chapter. While in Australia in 1967 in a public square in Brisbane, David made a decision that turned his life in a new direction.

Freshness, naturalness, and ease of conversation commended the gospel to those who heard David in Victoria, Queensland, Brisbane, Sydney, Melbourne, and other cities. The response was good everywhere he preached. In West Australia, aborigines made professions of faith. As a way to show his friendship to these Indians, David asked them to teach him some words in their language. He found out that *katukuto* means "cling on the highest"; *horana* means "place of peace"; *wengerup* is a "place of brotherhood."

The kookaburra bird so intrigued David that he wrote a column about it for the home missions magazine: "The kookaburra bird listens and laughs. It would be good for all of us if we could be like the kookaburra."

Occasionally Australian English confused David. For instance, he could not find a barber shop until Ray Taylor made clear a hair dresser and barber are one and the same.

Since the Australian Baptists had sent him a round-the-world ticket, individual churches did not give him an honorarium. At the last stop before Geelong, David realized the personal expense money he had brought along was about to run out but hesitated to ask his hostess for items such as shaving cream or tooth paste.

At the hotel in Geelong, he spent some time in prayer, asking God for some provision. That night at a supper meeting one man placed a five dollar bill in David's hand.

The next morning, speaking on radio, David mentioned the "Bible School of the Air" in Brazil, but asked for no money. A listener, one hundred miles away, sent him one hundred dollars by a traveler who was coming to town. In the afternoon, David visited a modern farm where he was given another one hundred dollars.

Then, as in Elisha's experience, the fountain dried up. No

more money was given him. What he had received was enough for his personal expenses the rest of the way home.

On a television show in South Australia, David announced that he intended to preach 120 minutes at the Baptist Tabernacle. When the temperature dropped to 35 degrees in "the sunny South," one pastor tried to discourage him in his plans to preach two hours.

"The meeting will be a failure. People won't come and stay that long in the cold."

Adelaide, on a plain between Mount Lofty and the sea, is divided by the Torrens River. Its North Terrace is one of the most beautiful streets anywhere, with flower gardens and lawns, mulga and gum trees, library, art gallery, and university. David could not help comparing the beauty of the city with the beauty of the spiritual experience at the tabernacle on Sunday afternoon.

In spite of the cold, a large crowd came, curious to hear the 120-minute sermon. All stayed to listen to the preacher with the strange accent.

At the close, the soloist sang "Out of My Bondage" more than ten times, and people were still coming to the front. Though the counselors were well organized, the chairman told David, "We have run out of counselors."

"Give two to each one."

On Wednesday night, David arrived in Brisbane, where quaint bungalows built on stilts and equipped with lattice screens to admit the breeze and temper the stifling heat lined the streets. The palm trees reminded David of Brazil.

Harry Orr, pastor of French's Forest Baptist Church, had been preaching in the revival crusade in the Baptist Tabernacle in Brisbane from Sunday through Wednesday. Thursday night David preached.

Friday, Orr invited David to eat lunch with him at the Canberra Restaurant on the square in Brisbane. Winding through the crowded streets, the two dodged pedestrians, young women with babies on their backs, young men in and out of coffee bars. Orr pointed out Lennon's Hotel, once General MacArthur's headquarters.

Hands on the tall clock tower at City Hall stood at twelve noon. In the restaurant two potato dishes were offered with the entree. David chose to try mutton.

"Tell me about your work," Orr insisted.

David told him about the radio program, the new church, his travels into the interior, and plans for home missions expansion.

"You have too much in your hands! You can't go on with all that!"

On the other side of the world from his problems, David could look at them more dispassionately. He realized the enormity of the task involved in the "Bible School of the Air" and the challenge of the Church of Hope.

At last he saw it was not possible to direct a work with 330 missionaries, be pastor of a church, preach on the radio twice daily, write the material for the radio program, teach a night class in theology, and be a good father and husband all at the same time. Something would have to go.

He prayed and received God's answer: "Give up the Board. I need you for another purpose."

Nothing was written to Haydee about the decision. But she did not act at all surprised when David told her upon his arrival at home.

"I alreay knew you were going to resign," she said. "While you were gone, God spoke to me too. I knew this would happen."

In November, 1967, David presented his resignation, effective June 12, 1968. At first the Board did not understand. They delayed for thirty days a vote to accept his resignation, but he knew there would be no change.

In a meeting at Fortaleza, Joao Soren asked the people to pray. He said, "I do not believe it is time for Gomes to leave the Board." David talked at length with his good friend Soren but knew in his heart there was no question. He felt at peace.

Within a day or so, the pastor who had wanted to know where David was putting all the money came to visit him and said, "You must not give up your work. We will just have to mobilize some people to help you and not let you leave."

"My decision was made at the feet of God. I thank you for

coming, but the day of my leaving is set."

The two continued talking until they reached the subject of money. "You know," David said, "the Board pays me 950 cruzeiros a month, and the church won't be able to pay me more than 250."

"They only pay you 950 cruzeiros?" the pastor asked in amazement. "I earn 1,200 and I'm just a helper on another Board."

David laughed, "They paid me what they wanted to. I don't have any regrets."

In the 14 years he had been executive secretary of the Home Mission Board the orphanages had increased from 1 to 2, the theological institutes from 1 to 2, the medical dispensaries from 3 to 14, the primary schools from 28 to 80, the number of missionaries from 100 to 330.

The Home Mission Board had raised its banner in fourteen states and in three territories. The work was further developed along the navigable part of the Sao Francisco River and along the new roads opened in the interior. Three young pastors were employed as associates in evangelism and education. New work was opened among several Indian tribes. The property of the Board was multiplied many times.

The budget for 1954 had been $375.00 or 1,200 cruzeiros. The budget for 1968 was $296,875.00 or 950,000 cruzeiros.

David sent out the following letter May 12, 1968: "God is the author of everything. I have served only as his instrument. I give God the praise and glory for that which God has permitted me to do, and I want to share it with my friends.

"I have marveled at the financial cooperation of the Brazilian people. The Lord worked and the people gave."

Samuel Mitt was elected as the new executive secretary of the Home Mission Board. He was a missionary director of the Baptist Theological Institute in Carolina, Maranhao, and had been called to home missions through David's ministry.

July 3, 1968, Harry Orr wrote from Australia: "It is now nearly twelve months since we met. I shall always value the fellowship we had in the Brisbane Tabernacle and the rich conversations we enjoyed with the good food provided by the Canberra.

"So now you are free from the double responsibility that exercised your mind so greatly when you were in Australia. . . . No man could continue at the pace you were going."

As pastor of Church of Hope, David turned down several invitations to become pastor of other churches, including the First Baptist Church of Sao Paulo. Invitations to preach in revivals and at conventions continued to come.

Not long after his resignation, he spoke in a section of the interior where he had spoken before. A group there told him, "We are surprised. We thought you would be sad, but you are still preaching with power!"

He answered, "I don't remember the past. I have work for the present. The Lord has given me a new heart." He held no resentment but was ready to go forward and not look backward.

The pieces in the kaleidoscope, the dark ones and the bright ones, were falling into formation in the hands of the One who held the instrument.

The old proverb was true: Sometimes God writes well with crooked lines.

Part III

The Fruit: 1969-1979

16

A New House

Seek ye first the kingdom of God, and his righteousness; and all these things shall be added unto you (Matt. 6:33).

Friends asked, "What will you live on?"

"God will provide, as always."

For a farewell gift the Board gave David and his family ten thousand cruzeiros. They would have to leave the house the Board had provided.

In family worship, one prayer request was for a house that would require no more than ten thousand cruzeiros down payment. One morning, while one of the children was praying thus, the phone rang.

A real estate agent said, "I have the right price house for you."

"Where is the house, Daddy?" Priscila asked.

When he told her the name of the street, far from their present address, she broke into tears. "Daddy, did you forget I have five courses to take? I couldn't live there and come to my classes. Did you think of that?"

She cried and cried until her father said, "We'll manage some other way. Don't cry any more. I won't buy that house. We can pile our belongings in one room at the Bible school headquarters and sleep in the auditorium until God shows us where to live."

At the time, the Bible School of the Air and the Church of Hope were one entity, their budget one. Later the church was constituted separately.

Hence, David planned to give the ten thousand cruzeiros to the Bible School Board as rent if the family could live at the church. He called the president of the Home Mission Board to explain this decision.

"I'm sorry, but you must not do this. The money was given to your whole family, not to you personally. I think you can find a wiser way to use it for the family."

That kind of straight talk gave him a shock. Yet he wondered what else to do.

Just when the Gomes family needed it most, another ten thousand cruzeiros came to them, this time from the Suman family estate. When Haydee's father died, he had left two houses in Curitiba. These had been up for sale for five years, but all the sisters and brothers could not agree on the matter of the final sale price. Several times Haydee had insisted she would give up her part of the property, but David told her, "We can't give up what doesn't belong to us. This is for the children."

Though Haydee's parents had died long before, only at this time when Haydee so badly needed the money did her family come to a settlement on how to divide their inheritance. Haydee's share was ten thousand cruzeiros.

Shortly after the second ten thousand cruzeiros had been deposited in the family treasury, an army major who had heard David preach in Parana called. He said, "A friend of mine is selling her apartment. Since she has seven children and you have six, I thought it might be the right size for you."

"Thank you, Major, but I'll have to pray about it first."

"Don't wait too long, for everybody wants it. It has not been advertised yet because I told my friend I'd like for you to have a chance to see it first."

When David had been praying for twenty minutes, Haydee phoned. She said, "David, I have an apartment for us. A major called and I have talked with the owner. The place is near the children's school, and we can't afford to lose it. We must go now."

Both of them liked the second-floor apartment at Rua Senador Furtado 62, Praca da Bandeira, next door to the Baptist headquarters. Its rooms were light, airy, and big enough for their family.

Haydee's favorite room was the blue and white tiled kitchen. Its large windows looked out into the courtyard at the center of the building, past an adjoining porch or balcony.

A small room previously used as servant's quarters would be ideal for a breakfast room, since they would probably not have a live-in servant. One bedroom had built-in bookcases. The owner, a woman, offered to include part of the furniture at a price of sixty-five thousand cruzeiros for everything. She wanted twenty thousand cruzeiros down payment.

David told her he was a minister and asked, "Would you allow me to read the Bible and my wife to lead in prayer before we leave?"

"I don't mind."

Afterward, the woman, accustomed to reciting prayers, requested, "Please write down this recitation for me."

Haydee told her, "I can't write this for you because it came from my heart. I just talked to God."

"Anyway, I appreciated it."

Later the same day a medical doctor offered cash for the apartment, but the woman told him, "I can't do that. A pastor was here. He read from the Bible and his wife said a prayer. I think the matter is settled."

Unusual for Brazil, because of fluctuation of money value, she set the rest of the payments in equal amounts of 547 cruzeiros a month, to be paid over six years. By the time David paid the last installment, the money (because of inflation) was about half the amount it was when he began paying, but the value of the apartment had tripled.

17

Letters from Listeners

He was given a regular allowance to cover his daily needs until the day of his death (Jer. 52:34, TLB).

"Ah, I know your voice! I listen to you on the 'Bible School of the Air,' " the pharmacist exclaimed as David walked into a drugstore in Rio.

From the beginning, the "Bible School of the Air" had resulted in thousands enrolled in Bible study through the correspondence courses and, judging from the letters received, in the salvation of hundreds of listeners.

In the program's twenty-ninth year, 110 programs were broadcast each week. Not only were programs carried on stations in Brazil but also on international stations, such as, Transworld Radio; Bonaire, Netherlands, Antilles; Voice of the Andes, Quito, Ecuador; Voice of the Cross, La Paz, Bolivia; The Friendship Voice, San Francisco.

In 1979, Radio Capital, the new station in Brasilia, added the program. Transworld Radio began broadcasting it in Swaziland, Africa. Almost anywhere in the world Portuguese was spoken, the "Bible School of the Air" could be heard in its thirtieth year, 1979.

Brazilians flying over the Amazon jungle or boating down the Tocantins River or sitting in their homes in Sao Paulo could hear the message of God's love by tuning in their radios. Letters came to the Bible School of the Air from all over Brazil and from as far away as Canada, and Baghdad, Iraq.

"I am the lost sheep," one man wrote. "Last night I heard you say that the ninety and nine are saved and the one sheep is lost. I am that one lost sheep. I write you now from the south to ask you how I can be saved."

Eunice Justino wrote:

You have had a very great influence in my life. I was a devout Catholic and 15 years ago, I became a believer. When I arrived in Rio, coming

126

from Minas Gerais, I began trying to win my large family to Christ.

I began to pray as did the church where I was a member—that God would show me a way to take the light of the Gospel to my family's farm away in the backwoods of the state of Minas Gerais, where there had never been until then any electricity or running water and where it had taken 24 hours walk to the nearest village. Today a bus goes there.

As I thought about my mother I would send her some tracts and other religious literature, but she could not believe in anything that was not Catholic. They had never heard that Christ is alive. . . . Then it was that God showed me a way in which I could help her understand Him. You will note that where my family lived there was no Baptist church.

On my mother's birthday, I decided to give her a little transistor radio as a present and told her of some of the programs she might enjoy hearing. Among the programs mentioned was yours—Bible School of the Air. The third time she listened to your program she was converted. Soon after her conversion, all of my family accepted Christ. From that moment on, the Bible School of the Air has been a sacred hour of worship and the whole household listens in complete silence.

Nineteen people in my family became Christians! A church was organized in the nearest town and today has more than 100 members. The most important thing, however, was God's infinite goodness placed in the message from your lips that reached my mother's heart and she was baptized on December 25, 1969, and on June 29, 1970, she was taken to be with our Lord.

My younger sister was crying . . . but my mother said, "Don't cry, my child. I am so happy. I am not going to die. I am going to rest." I cried when I received the message, but how grateful I was that God had permitted her to live until she had met her Saviour. For this reason, your influence has been very great in my life. The whole Justino family always prays for you and the Bible School of the Air.

Daisy Pirea de Sousa wrote:

It is with a great deal of pleasure that I send this letter for I wish to enroll in the Bible School of the Air.

I think I am of this religion, and ever since I began listening to your program, I began studying the Bible and have enjoyed the study very much. . . . I should like to become a Baptist. May I ask, please, if possible, if you will give me an explanation by correspondence about how prayer is said, by the use of rosary, and if you use communion and confirmation, for there is no Baptist church here. I should like to ask for three enrollment cards, one for me, one for my husband, and one for a 12-year-old daughter.

From Jaboatao, Pernambuco:

Mr. Professor, Reverend, and Friend:
I have just heard your program aired by Radio Continental of Recife. I have never found any religion that convinced me. I have been disappointed with all religions and philosophies. But it seems that you are right. I want to know your books and your denomination.
Signed, The Unknown Sinner

From Rio Claro, Sao Paulo: "*nao ha dinheiro que possa pagar.* There is no amount of money that could pay the value of what you said today. I want to study the Bible with you."

From Amazonia: "We have no church in our village, no school, nothing, but we have the Bible School of the Air. It is a great gift from God."

From Bahia: "Pastor, I want to be a Christian. I am 16 and have been hearing your program for three years."

From Teodosia Maria da Conceicao of Rio: "I am 74 years old. I have followed the Jehovah's Witnesses for many years, but now I have discovered that Jesus is Saviour, and they expelled me. I want a visit from you. I cannot leave home, for I am old."

From North Colombia: "I am a Catholic, a professor of religion. I would like Bible courses for myself and my class."

In 1953, a missionary, A. E. Blankenship, and two pastors on a mission tour of Santa Catarina ran across listeners to the "Bible School of the Air." This encounter turned into such an unusual event that Everet Gill, Jr. described it in his 1954 book, *Pilgrimage to Brazil.*

Blankenship and the three men were visiting places where there was no Baptist work. They traveled by station wagon equipped with a public address system.

The men met a couple who said they had been listening to a radio program with questions and answers about the Bible. David had advised his listeners to go to the nearest Baptist church if they wanted a Bible. This couple had ridden sixty miles to find a Baptist church. The community where they stopped happened to be where

Blankenship and his fellow workers had been forced to spend the night because of car trouble.

In the service, the couple listened eagerly to the preaching and the singing, never having heard anything like it before. After the service, they invited the missionaries to visit their home.

"The missionaries found a large crowd assembled," Gill wrote. "All the 'holy' pictures and images had been removed. For four hours they sang, prayed, and preached the Word of God. That night, 73 people confessed their faith in Christ."

Later, when the sixty Baptists in Urubici, in the mountains of Santa Catarina, held an evangelistic service with David as the preacher, they decided to try to fill the eight-hundred-seat theater for the service. They doubted it could be filled, but every seat was taken, including the balcony, and at least one hundred more standing in the aisles and doorways. There were twelve conversions.

Missionary Jesse Kidd said, "The 'Bible School of the Air' has done more for evangelization of Santa Catarina than any other agency I know about. It is certain there was prayer, preparation, and devotion of the church people. Also the people here in Urubici hear the daily radio programs." The fact that they were being led to read their Bibles was important.

Often a listener who accepted Jesus decided to throw away his idols and so took his crucifix to the Bible School of the Air headquarters. Soon David had bagfuls of crucifixes.

To the Bible questions-and-answers format, other features were added. Haydee began telling Bible stories for children. In her "Children's Hour," she gave her listeners a chance to enlist friends. In two days' mail, she received seven hundred names and addresses. A program for young people answered the questions in their letters, giving advice and counsel to help solve their problems. A news program, "To All the World," gave religious news briefs. A Portuguese translation of *Rosa's Quest* was offered free to anyone asking for it.

First Baptist Church of Burlington, North Carolina, gave a machine for taping the programs.

David, who had written the scripts from the beginning, continued to write them, as well as tape the programs himself. His salary for the radio work was nothing. He told the Bible School Board, "I don't want the money. I only want the blessings."

David never added another sponsor to the original one—God. Companies offered to pay large sums if he would endorse or advertise their products, but he refused all such offers.

He wrote several books and sold them, all profits to be used for broadcasting expenses. Two of his books were written from material from the "Questions and Answers from the Bible" program. Another was *A Jew Called Abraham*. In collaboration with Jabes Torres, David translated *The Gospel of Redemption* by W. T. Conner.

On May 23, 1978, David looked at the bank statement— 26,521 cruzeiros on deposit—and Bible school bills to be paid: 27,171 cruzeiros. By the following day, he had received the balance through an offering in the mail. Such an experience was repeated time and again.

For this reason, David had chosen as the theme verse of the radio programs Jeremiah 52:34: "And he was given a regular allowance to cover his daily needs until the day of his death."

Wherever David went he was always meeting his listeners. In March, 1977, he arrived in Sao Paulo in the pouring rain for a preaching engagement. He rode a crowded train part of the way to the church. Only fifteen minutes before time for the service, he stood under a cafe awning in the rain, trying to hail a taxi. But all taxis were taken. Finally he yelled to a passing car. The driver stopped, and he and his family drove David to the church. When the man saw David's card, he said, "I am your listener. I hear you at 3:30 every morning." Of eight converted that night, two said they had been listening to David on the radio.

In the depth of the jungle, he found families who listened to the "Bible School of the Air." Once, with twenty others, he was riding in an old truck on top of sacks of rice. When they were crossing a river, they saw a man catch a big fish, weighing about ten pounds. The driver asked the fisherman, "Would you sell us this?" The fisherman did, and the people on the truck dressed it.

When night fell, they stopped at the first house they saw. The family said the travelers could stay, but there was not enough food for so many. At that, the travelers produced the fish. While it was cooking, David heard the lady of the house call, "Daniel, come here." Later the father called the older son, "Silas, come here."

He thought then the family must be Christian, so he asked them if they were. The man answered, "Yes, we are Baptists." They had a battery radio and had been listening to the "Bible School of the Air."

Their guest said, "I am David Gomes." They hugged him and wanted to treat him like a king. They gave him the best hammock.

All the crowd ate the fish. Then David invited them all to join in a worship service. He had brought along one hymnal.

There were no electric lights—only one kerosene lamp, on a handmade table. David sat down by the lamp, opened his Bible, and preached the gospel. In the jungle the Lord made possible a happy time of Christian fellowship.

Years later, while David was at home one night in 1978, he got a telephone call. The Baptist preacher on the phone said, "I used to be one of your most severe critics, especially when you were with the Home Mission Board. Now God has used you to help me, and I want to thank you."

The pastor said that he and his wife had been having marital problems. In the middle of the night, his wife had turned the radio on, heard David speaking, and said to her husband, "Come and listen. He is talking to us." They prayed together and resolved their problems because of what they heard.

When visiting in Athens, Greece, David wanted to see the Acropolis. He sat down in the gardens of the Agora and waited. When a bus full of tourists stopped, he followed them and their guide to the top of the Acropolis. There he heard someone calling him. It was a young man serving in Israel with United Nations. "Hello, Pastor David," the young man said. "How is the 'Bible School of the Air'?"

18

The Miracle Lot

Jesus answering saith unto them, Have faith in God. For verily I say unto you, That whosoever shall say unto this mountain, Be thou removed, and be thou cast into the sea; and shall not doubt in his heart, but shall believe that those things which he saith shall come to pass; he shall have whatsoever he saith (Mark 11:22-23).

"It is not for sale."

The vacant corner lot next door held out a possibility for increasing the size of the Church of Hope building, but the owner of the 25 x 77 foot lot refused to sell it.

One Sunday in September, 1969, in response to an invitation from David, the owner attended a church service. As soon as he entered the narrow building, he exclaimed, "You are too crowded!"

"Then sell us your land!"

Though the man continued to refuse, David continued to pray that the man would change his mind.

David kept wondering how to make God known to the masses in downtown Rio. He continually turned over new ideas. A conventional type church with only Sunday and Wednesday night services might not reach all the types of people he knew were there—the tourists, the bankers, the lawyers, the navy personnel, the rich and the poor on the beaches and in the streets.

From the beginning, the Church of Hope stayed open Monday through Saturday from eight in the morning until six in the afternoon. Someone was always present to counsel, to witness, and to give out Bibles and other Christian literature. On Sundays and Wednesdays the hours were even longer. Daily noontime devotions were attended by gradually increasing numbers. Church members assisted in leading the daily noonday devotions.

Some people walked in from the city street who had never before entered a church. Many with problems came seeking help. Almost every day people made decisions to follow Christ. Some of these joined churches in other parts of the city or in distant states. Others joined the Church of Hope. As the membership grew, the building seemed to shrink. "Packed like sardines" described the congregation exactly.

On November 30, 1969, David went to Bogota, Colombia, for the First Latin American Evangelism Congress. Later he wrote in his journal, "God poured out His blessings on the Second Baptist Church of Bogota. And that night, in my room I heard a voice, 'I will give you the vacant lot.' "

Back in Rio, David wrote notes asking ten church members to meet with ten members of the Bible School Council to discuss the lot. The next morning a member of the Bible School Board called to tell David the owner of the lot was near bankruptcy and would probably be forced to sell.

On December 8, the owner told David he would sell the lot for $250,000. On December 23, David's birthday, the owner lowered the price to $175,000. That night after a Youth meeting in the church a young man remarked, "Now God has already paid $75,000. We dare not fail to come through with the rest."

More and more David realized how much this property could broaden the ministry of the "Bible School of the Air," as well as the church, and thus fulfill his yearning to make God known to more people.

David could envision a tall building on that lot on one of the busiest streets in the city. Besides the church, the building would house the studio for the "Bible School of the Air," a counseling center, a reading center, maybe a clinic, and a Bible school for all age levels. Offices could be used by Christian agencies, and additional space could be rented or leased to other companies and institutions.

The microscopic Church of Hope had no money to buy that valuable real estate—worth far more than the price quoted to the church—a piece of land that promised to grow in value as the city grew. Yet David, convinced he was doing what the Lord wanted him to do, began what he called a campaign of faith. He claimed God's promise in Mark 11:22-24: "And Jesus answered them, 'Have faith in God. Truly, I say to you, whoever says to this mountain, Be taken up and cast into the sea; and does not doubt in his heart, but believes that what he says will come to pass, it will be done for him. Therefore I tell you, whatever you ask in prayer, believe that you have received it, and it will be yours' " (RSV).

At the annual Brazilian Baptist Convention meeting in Bahia, David appealed for help. But the only money given him was twenty-five dollars from a Southern Baptist missionary who borrowed it from someone else. Neither the Brazilian Baptist Convention nor the Foreign Mission Board of the Southern Baptist Convention (to whom he also appealed for help) could single out the one church to aid when so many other churches and causes also demanded attention. However, the Brazilian Baptist Convention had twice endorsed the Church of Hope and the proposed building as a worthy mission project.

During the annual meeting in Rio, the Brazilian Baptist Loan Board was also meeting. David, a member of the Board, along with other pastors from all over the country, asked permission to speak.

He used as his text 1 Kings 18 where Elijah told Ahab that rain would surely come, though there was not a cloud in the sky. David pointed out that this was irrational thinking from the human standpoint; but in the light of Elijah's faith, it was perfectly logical. He went on to say that although neither he nor the Bible School of the Air nor the church had a cent to spare he knew that God was going to give the church the land. If necessary, God would work a miracle.

When he had finished speaking, one of the pastors prayed, thanking God for someone in the twentieth century who could see rain before clouds appeared.

As a result of that address, David was invited to preach and seek to raise money in Juiz de Fora, Brasilia, Sao Paulo, and Goiania. In Parque Jose Bonifacio, Rio de Janeiro, the Baptist church gave the first offering toward the purchase of the lot. In his own church, David continued to stress that money for purchasing the lot was to be over and above regular gifts to the Cooperative Program.

Over and over he appealed to other churches. He felt justified in doing this because he viewed the land as vital to increased evangelical work in Rio, a home missions ministry important to all Brazilian Baptists.

Others disagreed however. One pastor told him, "We need all the money we receive in order to reach our own church budgets."

In mid-March of 1970, David was told that the church definitely could have the land for $125,000 and would be given a thirty-day option. On April 1, the women of the church held a spiritual retreat. After three hours of prayer, they had a new awareness of the nearness of the Holy Spirit. All of the women, with tears of joy, resolved to give all they had—rings, bracelets, necklaces, and money.

At the end of the thirty-day option, the owner called to ask: "Do you have the money?"

"No."

"Do you still want the land?"

A definite yes. The church then had 130 members.

Six men gathered in the office of the owner—lawyers, the seller, and the would-be buyer. David opened the Bible to John 14:13 and read, "Whatsoever ye shall ask in my name, that will I do, that the Father may be glorified in the Son."

He said, "Men, you are about to witness a miracle, for God is going to give the church this land." He gave each of the men an offering envelope, saying, "This you may keep to show that you took part in a miracle, that you were a witness to what happened." One of the lawyers, Americo Nicolau de Oliveira, a member of Church of Hope, suggested that all of those present contribute ten cruzeiros to give the miracle a start; everyone did.

Then David confessed he had not brought enough money. But in the presence of those men, he prayed, "Lord, show us your power now by working this miracle."

The owner agreed to wait longer if the judge would allow it. Americo left to seek the judge.

Immediately David ran to the church where the daily prayer meeting was in progress. He stopped the service: "Let us all pray that the judge will extend our time." While all were kneeling in prayer, Americo rushed in to announce that the judge had granted ten more days.

In the very week of the new efforts to secure the property, Priscila, David's daughter, had developed a painful cough, and a fever. X rays showed she had tuberculosis in both lungs. At a church service, David, with tears coursing down his cheeks, told the congregation the doctor's diagnosis.

Members in deep anguish prayed for her daily. Tuesday, April 21, was set aside for a day of prayer for Priscila. Haydee, David, others of the family, and the church spent long hours on their knees. Finally at nine o'clock in the evening, David arose and told the others, "God is not sick. I believe he will both cure my daughter and give us the property."

When David got home at ten, Priscila greeted him at the door, weak, and feverish. It was a painful moment for the pastor, a moment when he felt that God was testing his faith.

Priscila's sleeping place was in the living room. Though David did not want to leave her, around midnight he went to his room. From there he heard her coughing and coughing. At his bedside, he knelt and pleaded, "Lord, please extend your hand. Stop her from coughing. Help her to sleep."

She did not cough again the rest of the night. The next morning she awoke refreshed, with color in her cheeks. She seemed so much better that her father took her to the National Tuberculosis Center to have a new X ray made.

The doctor rejected the first X ray and ordered another. When he looked at the second X ray, he called his colleagues and asked, "Could my diagnosis have been wrong? I don't know what has happened, but this X ray shows a complete cure."

One of the doctors looking at the X ray said, "This could only happen once in a hundred years to the son of a priest!"

David interrupted to make plain that this was a miracle of God. In the doctor's office, he praised the Lord.

On April 24, an attorney called to say the money must be in hand for the land by Monday, April 26. A quiver of alarm touched David. The time was too short.

In the Bible School of the Air paper, *Noticias Escobar*, he had published a statement once that the most effective prayer is the prayer of acquiescence. Now he knew he had to pray that kind of prayer.

As he sat down to prepare his sermon for Sunday, April 25, David wanted to cry. How could he face the people who had already given sacrificially and generously?

He thought of the drawing that the artist, Milton de la Cadona, had given him. It showed a tiny Faith Center on the land where the present church building was. It seemed that the drawing would be prophetic.

David had pleaded long with God, but finally he gave up insisting on his own way: "If you don't want us to have the lot, Lord, I give it up." Weeping harder than ever before in his life, he said, "Lord, show me how we can use the small building we have."

When he regained his composure, David wrote God a letter and told him of his acquiescence. He signed and sealed it.

Sunday morning when David arrived at church, Priscila, the pianist, was playing the prelude, a hymn, "My eternal possession—my Saviour—is more to me than love, or life itself. My God is more to me than anything I know."

That morning David said to the congregation, "Jesus is worth much more than any piece of land. We have him. If God had willed it, we would have obtained the money for the property." As David had acquiesced, he led the congregation to do the same.

He told those present, "The church is God's representative on earth. I will give you this letter if you will accept it without knowing its contents. Tomorrow we will tell the judge we don't have the money."

Many were in tears. David gave the deacons his letter to God; the church members, on their knees, accepted his decision.

Yet that night he said to Haydee, "I don't believe we have lost the property."

She looked at him in astonishment. "I don't understand you. You gave it up this morning, and now you say you didn't lose it."

"I've been thinking. Did you doubt God was going to answer our prayers?"

"No, I did not doubt."

"I didn't doubt either, and the Lord said in Mark 11 that if you have faith in God anything in the world will be given you; even the mountains will be cast into the sea. We have faith in God. We don't doubt his Word. The Lord will give us the property! Let's praise him for it." They both thanked God, for they knew the answer would come, though they did not know how.

On Monday, the appointed day, the judge did not contact them.

Early on May 1, a national holiday, David appealed to listeners of the "Bible School of the Air," asking them to bring gifts to the church.

All day crowds of people kept coming and going, poor people bringing old and new belongings. Two men delivered an antique sewing machine. Others gave kitchen utensils, watches, wedding rings, bracelets, money, and pledges. One boy contributed a bicycle.

David ate lunch at the church and stayed until 7:30 in the evening. As soon as he had turned out the lights, he heard someone knocking. It was another group with more gifts.

Still the total was far from enough. Faith, though, does not look at mountains. It looks at the God who moves mountains.

That night a man suggested, "Why don't you call Joseph Souza Marques, of the House of Representatives? He is a Baptist pastor, and I think he will lend some money."

David tried to call, but the phone went dead. Souza Marques lived in Jacarepagua, on the other side of Rio. But before David could complete the call or leave to go there, Souza called him.

Souza promised, "I will lend you one hundred thousand cruzeiros at no interest." This was a third of the amount needed.

On the next Thursday, one of the lawyers called to see if the church had the money.

"Not yet, but we will have it."

"You're going to lose that land, Pastor," the lawyer said. "Monday will definitely be your last chance."

"God created the world in six days," David told the lawyer, "so he can give us this little piece of land in four, can't he?" He had confidence in his heart that he could not explain to anyone else.

Monday morning, May 11, his office phone was still out of order. He spent the morning in prayer. At noon, he lunched at home with his family. The lawyer called him there to set up an afternoon appointment.

At three o'clock, the lawyer asked, "Did you bring the money?"

"Perhaps one of the nearby banks would give us a loan," came the last straw reply.

"We can try," the lawyer asserted.

"Let's pray first."

"Pastor, we have two hours. Are you going to waste our precious time praying?"

"Don't worry. It will only take a moment."

"Which bank shall we try?"

David, unaware that the lawyer was a friend of the president of the Boa Vista Bank and had already talked with him, answered, "Let's try the Boa Vista. A member of our church council has had pleasant business dealings with the president."

The president of the bank asked, "Are you the man who has been speaking on the radio about getting a lot?"

"Yes sir."

"Have you paid for it yet?"

"No, but I came here to get the money for it from your bank."

The president, Fernando Machado Portella, replied, "But you have no account here."

"I will open one today with the three hundred thousand cruzeiros you will lend me."

"Who will vouch for you?" the president inquired.

"God," David replied.

"I need someone to sign the papers."

At that moment, the lawyer asked, "Could I vouch for him?" The lawyer said he wanted to sign because he was glad to find a man who believed in miracles.

The banker said, "A miracle has taken place here." It was ten minutes before the appointed deadline.

With only minutes left to deposit the money, the elated David did not forget to praise God. He invited everyone in the adjoining bank offices to a season of prayer in the president's office. He did not miss an opportunity to witness to the goodness of the Lord of his life.

David signed the papers and ran downstairs to deposit the money. The Lord had done a marvelous thing!

At the old church building on Primeiro de Marzo Street, the custodian was sweeping the floor. When he heard of the miracle, he fell on his knees and wept tears of joy.

From the church, David hurried home. Dorine Hawkins and Sophia Nichols were there with Haydee and the children. David walked in and shouted, "We have bought the property!" Everyone was astonished. They all formed a prayer circle to offer thanksgiving to God. Sophia Regina prayed, "Lord, thank you for not allowing us to doubt."

19

Gideon's Three Hundred

The Lord said unto Gideon, By the three hundred men that lapped will I save you, and deliver the Midianites into thine hand (Judg. 7:7).

David could not stop talking about the miracle of the vacant lot. On a plane to Rio Grande do Sul, he told the story to everyone he met. An engineer on his way to Concordia marveled. A Catholic nun asked if David would accept her gift of five dollars.

Interest at about fifty dollars a day kept adding up, though. All the loans from churches and individuals and banks needed to be repaid as soon as possible. Gifts kept coming in, but they were only paying the interest. The debt itself was not decreasing.

A church barbecue for "liberation from debt" sold food at a dollar a plate. When the meat and charcoal were paid for, barely three hundred dollars was left in profit. This was not the way to pay for the land, David knew.

Though he believed the purchase of the land had been done only with God's help, he still felt a weight of responsibility. Often he gave way to worry and depression, as he saw the impossibility of paying such a debt. In early 1971, he began to lose sleep.

Haydee would ask, "Are we really paying the debt?"

If he said no, she would be disturbed. If he said yes, that would be a lie. So he would change the subject and say, "Let's thank God because the offerings are coming." He did not say that the offerings were usually smaller than the interest owed each month. So Haydee went to sleep while David lay awake and worried.

He began what he called "nights of faith." He spoke in churches, with their permission, and took an offering for the land. Usually the offering no more than paid his travel expense to the church. At one convention meeting, he poured his heart out to a packed house. The offering was thirty dollars.

David was frankly told by one pastor that his church did not need another offering appeal. He said many others in their

141

churches felt the same. Another pastor told David, "We don't like to give an offering for a project we don't really know much about."

However, one young woman who heard David speak sold her new Ford to give the proceeds to the Church of Hope. She said that her father had been won to Christ by David's father.

David had not planned to go to the meeting of the Brazilian Baptist Convention in Campos. But as he was driving home in his old car, he suddenly felt that he should. From Rio he rode the bus for five hours, found an inexpensive hotel, washed his face, changed his shirt, and walked to the church.

It was foreign missions night. As he entered, Alcides Telles de Almeida, executive secretary of the Foreign Mission Board, announced, "Here is David Gomes. I will ask him to tell us about the miracle lot." David definitely felt God was in this, for he had not even planned to attend the meeting.

As he finished speaking, David got a note from Joseph Underwood of Richmond, Virginia, of the Foreign Mission Board, SBC. Underwood was a friend of many years, who was in the audience.

Next day at his hotel Underwood said, "David, as you were speaking, I thought you should be the liaison man for the coming reconciliation campaign of the Baptist World Alliance. Let's pray about that."

"Well, Joe, anything to help evangelize the world, I am ready to do."

A few months later he met with Underwood and other Baptist World Alliance leaders in Washington, DC. While in Washington, he decided to ask some friends of his in the United States if they would like to help with the payments on the lot. He bought a Trailways bus ticket that would take him anywhere in the States for ninety-nine dollars. Though he traveled to Oklahoma and back to Miami, stopping along the way, he got little money.

One morning while reading his Bible, he noticed Lamentations 3:24: "The Lord is my portion." That clung to him for the rest of the journey. It was consolation in a time of discouragement.

Back in Brazil, he went with Haydee and his whole family to the state of Espirito Santo to speak. Five churches met together.

There were confessions of faith and rededications, but the offering hardly paid his gas bill from Rio.

Tossing in bed that night David thought, *Lord, I admit I have been wrong. This is not the way.*

In Espirito Santo, he visited the pastor, Joao Gomes de Oliveira. As they stood talking under an orange tree, the pastor said, "You need to start a new campaign and call it "Gideon's Three Hundred." How much do you owe?"

"More than three hundred thousand cruzeiros."

"Then ask three hundred to give one thousand each. If you have three hundred giving one thousand cruzeiros, you have enough to pay the bank."

They prayed together under the orange tree, and David told the pastor, "I think this is from God."

Next day the Gomes family drove all day back toward Rio. Crossing from Niteroi on the ferry, David turned the radio on, and heard a man preaching about Gideon's three hundred. He told Haydee, "This was suggested to me this morning, and I have prayed about it the whole day. I think this is a confirmation from God. The radio speaker is talking about Gideon's three hundred! I am going to organize 'Gideon's Three Hundred!'"

David was surprised to discover how many people wanted to be Gideons. David prepared diplomas for the ones who would give a thousand cruzeiros (three hundred dollars). Of the three hundred Gideons, forty were from America. Three or four persons gave much more than three hundred dollars.

With the Gideon campaign, David started paying the principal, not just the interest on the loan. Other radio listeners and church members continued to give. A beggar brought six dollars; a young man brought his bicycle which sold for fifty dollars. A fourteen-year-old worked until midnight and got up at six to make dolls to sell so she could give her money. A ten-year-old gave two dollars, a birthday gift from her father. When her father asked why she gave her whole gift, she said, "Father, you give your all. I want to give my all."

The church had borrowed from individuals and from several

different banks to meet interest payments. When suddenly one creditor asked that his four hundred dollars be paid in full within twenty-four hours, Haydee checked all the banks, but the church had only eighty dollars on deposit.

Since women were at the church for a day of prayer for foreign missions, she thought of asking them to pray about this problem, but she heard God's admonition, "Daughter, I will provide the money. Be still." She did not say anything to the women.

Next morning, she sold some empty bottles for seventy dollars. Early in the day, a couple visited the Bible School of the Air for the first time and gave eighty dollars. By the end of the day, the four hundred dollars had come, plus twenty cents.

By November, 1971, three churches that had provided loans had been paid. The Bank of Sao Paulo was paid; the Banco Credito Real was paid. Banco Boa Visto had been paid one third.

By mid-1972, the Church of Hope could see that the miracle lot was to be a reality, a gift from God to be used for his glory.

But another fight was about to begin. The title for the land was not clear. The property had been mortgaged by the bankrupt company to the INPS (a department of the government). To get the deed, the church was told it would have to pay off the mortgage.

20

A Bold Witness

Be ready always to give . . . a reason of the hope that is in you (1 Pet. 3:15).

All the time plans were being made to buy the vacant lot, the Church of Hope continued to grow. The Engenho de Dentro Church, where David had once been assistant pastor, gave the church some of its old pews. Marcos David Gomes and some of the other young men painted the church ceiling.

Seeking creative, innovative ways to reach more people, as well as ways to increase the Bible knowledge of the members, David started a series of marathons. The first was reading the Bible aloud straight through from beginning to end.

In December, 1970, David learned that it was possible to read the Bible aloud in eighty hours. He mentioned this in his sermon on Sunday morning and told the church members he thought they could do it.

At lunch that day Haydee told him, "I hope you won't ask the church to do this. If it didn't work out, everybody would be embarrassed."

But when he got to the church that night, everybody was talking about reading the Bible through in eighty hours. There was nothing for him to do but set a date.

He listed several rules. First, the marathon was to be a time of worship. Only believers would read the Bible. Second, no young man could read unless he wore a tie. Since some did not wear ties, David brought a stack of them to the church so every young man who got up to read could wear one. Third, the reading would be organized by groups named for Bible characters, such as Moses and Paul, or for important persons, such as Ferreira de Almeida, the first man who translated the Bible into Portuguese. Each group would have ten members, including a chairperson. Groups would succeed each other, reading two and one-half hours each.

A committee was appointed to keep the time schedule and to watch the time limit on each one's reading. Every group took a long break before coming to read again. Some went home to rest while others stayed. Visitors who were believers were permitted to read if they wished to do so. Many from different churches came to take part, or to listen.

Some church members were always on the corner at the bus stop in front of the church, inviting people on the street to come in to hear the Bible reading.

One church member and the pastor stayed for the whole eighty hours. David would stay in the sanctuary five hours, sleep twenty or thirty minutes, and return for five more hours, so that he made it all the way through.

Between the Old and New Testaments someone rang a bell to give the idea of changing from the old to the new, to add drama and to give color.

The whole church was so uplifted by the marathon that everybody kept asking for another. Several months later the church met to sing through the whole hymnal, 578 hymns in 30 hours. Choirs for all ages had been organized, plus an orchestra.

David sent press releases to radio and television stations, reporting that the congregation would sing hymns by Mendelssohn and Mozart. He knew which hymns were set to music by these, so when newsmen came and asked about the hymns of Mendelssohn, he showed them the hymns in the book.

All the main newspapers of Rio sent reporters. Two major television stations showed news spots of the marathon. Radio Globe broadcast much of the singing.

"When a marathon can attract attention of newsmen in Sao Paulo and mobilize the whole press of Rio, it is because God has opened the doors!" David told a missionary friend.

When the singers were nearing the end of the hymnbook, a man, half-drunk, staggered into the church and asked to say a word. He was told nobody could speak—just sing. But he persisted until he gained permission to speak.

"I came to bring an offering," he said, "of a thousand cruzeiros. I was enrolled in church many years ago, but I left the church and forgot it. Tonight we were eating supper at my house with the television on. When I heard you singing I decided to bring my offering and tell you I have come back to God."

During the singing marathon, groups were assigned certain lengths of time as before. Always extras stayed on standby in case anyone failed, but all showed up at the proper times. Always at least one hundred were present. An eighteen-year-old girl and her group came at 3 AM. Then Dorine Hawkins (Stewart), missionary director of the Girls' Training School, brought students at 4 AM. She lighted a candle and started the singing. Then girls lighted their candles from hers and walked across the church with the lighted candles. They walked out onto the vacant lot and circled it with their lights, singing as they went.

A second Bible reading marathon lasted seventy-two hours. Almost to the end of Revelation, at 1:15 AM, David saw a girl crying. He asked, "Angela, what is wrong?"

"Pastor, there is no more Bible to read." She had been in the church for the whole seventy-two hours.

Later the Baptist Convention of Sao Paulo decided to have a Bible reading marathon similar to the one at the Church of Hope. While Baptists in Sao Paulo read the whole Bible aloud in an open square of the city, the governor of the state came to listen.

Then in Brasilia also the entire Bible was read aloud in a public square. Several government ministers assisted in the reading. To Brazilian Baptists, this was a great thing because in earlier years Bible reading in the country had been forbidden or suppressed.

During the Southern Baptist Convention in Norfolk, Virginia, in 1976, the idea of reading the Bible in seventy-two hours was referred to The Sunday School Board. A marathon—singing through the hymnal—was used in Nashville to present the new *Baptist Hymnal* in 1975. This idea has also been used in Australia.

Next, the church had a marathon of the Ten Commandments, a sermon on each Commandment. The congregation stayed in church from ten in the morning until ten at night, a packed house the whole time.

Because the number of Commandments is ten, David had picked the hour of ten to start and close the marathon. He often used dates or numbers in this way to dramatize challenges. He had prepared ten sermons, one on each Commandment, just in case he was needed, but all the other preachers came, and he didn't get a chance to preach any of them.

After the sermon, "Thou Shalt Not Kill," a man in the audience stood to say, "Pastor, I have been a member of the church for eight years, but hate, suspicion, and violence have prevented me from having Jesus in my life. Tonight I come to him. I cannot continue the kind of life I have been living."

Besides the marathons, the Church of Hope found other creative ways to reach out. On the Friday before Easter, church members and the choir walked in parade around a public square, around the church, and then a mile and a half farther. People of all ages joined the parade. As they marched, they stopped to talk to people along the street about the risen Christ, the reason for celebration of Easter. As a result, at least two made professions of faith. One of those joined the Church of Hope.

Missionaries for a day were sent out to cities with no Baptist work. The church would rent buses and almost everyone in the church would go spend a day preaching and witnessing in a chosen city. The second year this was done, thirty people were converted in one city.

Daily devotions at noon kept increasing in the number attending. Hardly a day passed without a profession of faith in this service. The brilliant lawyer, Americo Nicolau de Oliveira, led a devotion one day a week.

One Monday two bank directors attended the noonday meeting, one of whom had never owned a Bible. David gave the banker a New Testament and that afternoon visited him in his office to talk at length about Christ.

As anticipated, the church, open every day from 8 AM to 6 PM, attracted the seamen and navy personnel in the area, as well as tourists of many nationalities. Among the first Americans to visit were Owen Cooper, Glendon McCullough and Alma Hunt, leaders of the Southern Baptist Convention. All countries were as near as the main pier and shipping dock only a few blocks away. Regularly citizens of other nations visited the church. Soon David saw a need for services in English, Japanese, French, and Spanish, but he had no ministers available to conduct them.

During the week, a retired minister or a church committee stayed at the church to counsel with those who came in and asked for help. Many who came in from the street were people with great needs, some with desperate needs, some ready to commit suicide. Often they could be led to an acceptance of Christ.

By 1971, when the church was five years old, the membership was near two hundred. With an average per member income of only a hundred dollars a month, the congregation of generous givers was supporting a pastor, giving to the Cooperative Program, and giving to special missions offerings and to the Bible School of the Air.

In 1974, from May to August, seventy persons accepted Christ, in services sponsored by the church. During June and July that year, the Church of Hope directed an average of three meetings a day in homes, public squares, jails, and other places, in addition to the regular services at the church.

Preaching points established by the church on a continuing basis included one in the vacation home of the lawyer, Oliveira, at Petropolis in the mountains north of the city. Of four missions the church had started, two were called Faith and Love. Later preaching points were started as Pass Quatro, 150 kilometers from Rio, and at Cruzeiro.

Within a few years, as many as eighty thousand may be living in a housing project near the church. The next street over from the First of March is the broad Avenue Vargas, which terminates in the Catholic cathedral, Candelaria (the cathedral is a block to the right of the church). The housing project is to be continued down both sides of Vargas.

Once a quarter an all-night prayer meeting is held at Church of Hope. In early 1979, the church began an unusual type of revival meeting with a watch night of prayer. On a Monday night, 120 stayed to pray from 11 PM until 6 AM.

Then for four days, Tuesday through Friday, five-hour services were held every afternoon from two until seven o'clock, with five different preachers every day.

Twenty preachers had been asked to take part. In the twenty hours of preaching, each of the twenty preachers had an hour each. Every day, five preachers spoke, one after the other. One would preach and give an invitation. The congregation would sing. The another preacher would deliver his message and give an invitation, and so on, until all five had finished. Five invitations were thus given in the course of the five-hour meeting. During the four days, fifty-six accepted Christ, most of whom lived in other cities and did not place their membership in the Church of Hope.

During that week of revival, sixteen thousand leaflets were distributed, some in the services, others on the streets. The following week three people came with leaflets in hand—one from Parana, three hundred miles away—asking information on how to become a Christian.

On August 14, 1979, the church celebrated its thirteenth anniversary with a thirteen-hour prayer meeting. Again David used numbers to challenge members to take part in an activity. When the thirteen hours, plus thirty minutes had passed, many still did not want to go home.

A "Love of God" phone service was inaugurated at the church to accept calls from the desperate and the needy and to offer advice and comfort.

On a typical Sunday morning in the church's thirteenth year, the members enter at 7:30 or 8, sit down and pray quietly for a few moments. Then the young people pray together in one corner, or in a room upstairs. Several women sit in another corner, praying. The men are in another part of the building, engaged in an early prayer meeting. A sense of expectancy and urgency pervades the place.

As Sunday School begins about nine, the classes meet in every accessible spot. Mariruth and Fred Hawkins, missionaries, are among the Sunday School teachers.

In a tiny kitchen upstairs, a few women are discussing lunch plans. Most of the members will stay at the church or in the downtown area all day and on into the night, and many will eat lunch here. Each family has brought a dish as a contribution. All will pay a small sum for the lunch so that the profit can be applied toward the church's future building cost.

About ten o'clock, a children's choir assembles at the front of the sanctuary and begins to sing choruses. On the tables behind them are white lace tablecloths and four bouquets of fresh red roses.

Geremias, the associate pastor, makes the announcements and reads the communications from former members, plus wedding invitations and birthday celebration invitations. (In Brazil, it is the custom for those having birthdays to ask the pastor to conduct a worship service thanking God for allowing them to live another year. Hundreds who would never go inside a church at any other time will gladly attend such a birthday celebration.)

Visitors are introduced from the United States, Paraguay, Chile, Colombia, and several states in Brazil.

It is steamy hot; fans blow on those at the front near the piano. Marcos, David's son, an engineer, adjusts the sound system. His wife, Deisee, is the pianist.

Offering envelopes are given to those who request them, and ushers collect the offering in velvet bags. David reads 1 John 1:7: "If we are living in the light of God's presence, just as Christ does, then we have wonderful fellowship and joy with each other, and the blood of Jesus his Son cleanses us from every sin" (TLB).

Esther Ruth leads a young women's ensemble in special music. A young man sings a solo.

The sermon is not a quickly-prepared thought, but as John Marrs, American Baptist missionary said:

It is the essence of many years of walking with the Lord in the power of his Spirit. When David preaches, lives are touched. The Holy Spirit is speaking through him in a remarkable way.

The church is alive, but in no way superficial. The people just love the Lord and sing and pray with their whole hearts.

David has great discernment and is able to say a word at the right time. After the invitation and the people are leaving, he often speaks to an individual and then calls a deacon or other Christian worker who in turn perhaps leads the individual to saving faith in Jesus.

The lunch is as good as the delectable smells from the kitchen had promised: roast beef, rice and beans, ground beef spiced with a hot sauce, lettuce and tomato salad, potato salad, then baked bananas for dessert.

It's a long way home for most members, so they stay at church all afternoon. Some go to preaching points in the *favelas* or to others of the church's missions. David visits church members for an hour or two, then rests and studies, and goes back to the sanctuary for the evening service.

From seven to nine the congregation sings, listens to testimonies, and hears another sermon. Guests are present who did not come to the church in the morning.

The invitation hymn is "Footsteps of Jesus," translated into Portuguese by David when he was in Miami in 1965. Fifteen persons crowd forward to make professions of faith. Geremias and Elizabeth, David's youngest daughter, talk with the converts, writing down their names.

At the close of the service, all sit down again to pray silently once more before leaving, as is a custom in all Brazilian Baptist churches.

Then all rise and leave joyfully, singing as they go.

21

Mount Moriah

In thy seed shall all the nations of the earth be blessed; because thou hast obeyed my voice (Gen. 22:18).

May Day, 1974, Haydee and David drove to the Baptist Orphanage on the edge of Rio. As they returned home, they saw a man by the side of the road, his tables and wheelbarrows loaded with oranges and other fruits for sale.

"Haydee, let me buy you an orange," David offered.

"Where did you get these fruits?" he asked the vendor.

"From my farm," the man indicated the mountainside acreage across the road.

"You are a wealthy man if you own that!"

"I want to sell the land but don't have a buyer yet."

Only the month before, a nurse for the Exxon Petroleum Company had died, leaving forty thousand cruzeiros to the Bible School of the Air. She had been converted through the radio ministry.

Besides that donation, the widow of Moses Silveira, a former executive secretary of the Foreign Mission Board, Brazilian Baptist Convention, had given fifty thousand cruzeiros to the Bible School of the Air as a memorial to her husband.

This ninety thousand cruzeiros David had not wanted to place in the general expense fund but had wanted something that would be more tangible and memorable. He had prayed he might find a wise use for the money.

At that time, the Church of Hope and Bible School of the Air were still one unit legally. As David looked at the land, he felt it would be a good investment. Within a few days, he planned to leave for the United States where Sophia Regina was to enter Gardner-Webb College. Baptist Men of North Carolina had offered her a full scholarship. Hence, he gave the farmer his card and told him to contact the lawyer of the Bible School of the Air.

"Oh, I hear your radio programs often," the man said.

When David got back from the USA, Haydee told him, "We have bought the property for 120,000 cruzeiros." The 90,000 had paid three-fourths of the price for the 220,000 square meters of land.

That night, under a weight of guilt, David lay awake thinking, *Why did I waste the money this way? What do I need with land? I am not a farmer.* Finally he got up and walked into the living room where he sat and prayed, "Lord, I want to know if I have made a mistake. Forgive me if I have."

Suddenly came an unbidden thought: *Make that an encampment of faith. Call it Mount Moriah.*

David could visualize the shape of the tract of land. It was narrow at one end and wide at the other, symbolic of one entering a wide road or a narrow road. Also it resembled someone kneeling with hands lifted in prayer. Or it could be thought of as a big communion cup. This could be the logo of the camp.

He heard a voice saying, "This will be used for the edification of my people." He praised God and went back to bed to sleep soundly.

When he woke up long after the sun had risen, Haydee asked, "Why did you sleep so late?" He did not tell her the reason.

Now that he knew the land would be a camp, he returned to look at it with new eyes. He wanted to be able to describe it to the church and to the radio listeners.

He could see that he had bought a beautiful piece of real estate. Fruit trees dotted the lower levels—mangos, cashews, oranges, bananas, japoticabas. Fruit could be sold as camp income or used to supplement the campers' diet.

The level terrace midway up the mountain would be a good place for a future chapel if a stone wall were built to sustain the earth. Portraits of the nurse and of Moses Silveira should be hung in the chapel. For the present, this level spot would be great for soccer and volleyball.

Rounding the edge of a slope, David came to the brink of a cup-like hollow which formed a sort of natural amphitheater, boulders lying in a semicircle as if placed there for seats. A taller rock at the center was the right height for a pulpit. *This will be the Chapel of Stone,* he thought, *for outdoor services.*

He climbed on toward the top of the mountain. Almost at the summit, he found a tremendous granite slab. *Here we will build a Tower of Prayer with a lighted sign: "Jesus Is Coming, Let Us Be Praying." It will be seen by travelers on the highway below, the traffic from Rio to Sao Paulo.*

Mount Moriah would be a place for church retreats and for university student groups to meet in the summer. It could be a mission point from which to reach people in the surrounding community, as well as an influence on those who came to camp events.

Immediately Church of Hope members, the Bible School Board and others set out to ready Mount Moriah for use. In the beginning, the eight old chicken houses were dorms, their long windows open to the sky and mats on the concrete floor, the only beds.

Plans were made for three buildings to be called Faith, Hope, and Love. First Baptist Church, Crystal Springs, Mississippi, sent a thousand dollars to help pay for one. An apartment was furnished in one of the two dwelling houses as a home for the caretaker. One woman gave furniture for the main building. A piano was delivered as a memorial gift.

Still, the kitchen needed a stove, so Haydee cooked and sold meals at the Church of Hope every day for a week. Her profit of $112 bought the stove.

Then June 17, 1976, the camp opened for the first worship service. David described it as "God on earth."

They formed a human chain from the top of the mountain property to the bottom. As they held hands, they each said a prayer. Then, as only enthusiastic young Brazilians can sing, they raised their voices to the heavens: "Glory, glory, hallelujah, our God is marching on."

Across the valley on the next mountaintop lived a family in a little hut. When they heard the magnificent music, they came out to investigate its source. They walked down one hillside and up another until they found the young people and asked why they were singing.

"Because we love Jesus, and he loves us, and he loves you."

As a result, every member of that family accepted Jesus as Savior.

Mount Moriah was a popular place from the start, especially with young people. During more than one singspiration at the Chapel of Stone, the musicians climbed into the trees while the singers sat on the rocks below them.

Fred Hawkins and David led evangelism conferences for a retreat during carnival season. In 1977, YWA girls came from all over the state of Rio de Janeiro for a week. Then pastors and deacons gathered for a meeting sponsored by the Board of Evangelism.

Occasionally travelers on the highway stopped to visit the camp. Some of them had heard David describe the place on radio. In the same way, radio listeners and other travelers from the interior had visited the Church of Hope, as they happened to be passing by it during the week.

A regular Bible study group started at the camp by residents of the community. This grew into the first mission of the Church of Hope, now organized as a congregation with eighty members. Soon it will become a regular church.

In 1979, a new dorm for 50 people was completed, giving the camp the capacity to lodge 260. One evening when 200 campers were present, a camp fire was built at the site of the future chapel and a loudspeaker installed.

"God wants to kindle a fire," David told the campers. He quoted from Ezekiel 20:47-48: "Thus saith the Lord God; . . . I will kindle a fire in thee, and it shall devour every green tree in thee, and every dry tree: the flaming flame shall not be quenched. . . . And all flesh shall see that I the Lord have kindled it."

David continued, "God will cut down the green and the dry. The green are the immature of spirit; the dry are those with unfruitful use of their capacities. We are not to be as children tossed like ships (Eph. 4:14), or like 'clouds . . . without water' (Jude 12). We are to have objectives in life, and high ideals."

Then he focused on the light that shines. "Jesus said we Christians are 'salt' and then 'light.' Never the reverse. The shine of our lives is connected with the will of God (Rom. 12). When we are in his will there is no way to cut out our light; it will spread all over the nations. And all men will know God did it and not us."

He closed with a quotation from Moody: "The world has yet to see what God can do with a man entirely dedicated to him."

All present but three came forward to rededicate their lives. And one girl, Rosemaria, a spiritist, said she wanted to leave her old ways and follow Jesus.

A woman, who had listened to the "Bible School of the Air," died and left money to help build the chapel at the camp. Volunteers from Florida and Texas, in 1980, went to Brazil and built the chapel that David had envisioned. Its aluminum roof can be seen by travelers on the highway from Rio to Sao Paulo.

22

Star Witness

Ye are the light of the world; . . . let your light so shine (Matt. 5:14,16).

In 1977, a young Anglican minister visited G. S. Freeman, general superintendent of the Baptist Union of Western Australia, and indicated a desire to join the Baptist ranks at West Perth. He had already resigned from the Church of England.

As Freeman asked the young man about the decision to become a Baptist, he explained that in the state of Victoria, two hundred miles away, he had heard an address ten years before by "David Gomes from Brazil."

The young minister said, "His English wasn't very good, but he said what I needed to hear."

*   *   *   *

While Debbie Trott, missionary kid, was a student at Mississippi College, she took her junior year in France. She attended a Baptist church in Toulouse.

One Sunday morning a man came to church who could speak only Portuguese. Church members knew Debbie was the daughter of Edd and Freda Trott, missionaries to Brazil, so they asked her to translate the French service to Pedro Louis Alvaro.

Pedro asked her, "Do you know David Gomes?"

"Yes," Debbie answered. "I know him well."

"His signature is in my Bible." Pedro opened the Book to show her. He explained that David had won him to Christ during an evangelistic crusade in Portugal.

"I had many family problems," he said. "Pastor Gomes talked to me every day he was in our city. He really showed me that he cared about me, and so I felt that God cared about me too."

*   *   *   *

David is so full of the joy of living and has such a wide variety of interests himself that he finds it easy to establish rapport with others. In witnessing, he takes the initiative to ask questions, to draw people out, learn their names, their interests, their concerns.

He was flying to Manaus when the flight attendant brought his tray.

"My, you are a pretty girl!" he teased. "What is your hometown?"

"Curitiba."

"I know that city. My wife came from there. I am a missionary." He referred to his years as director of the Home Mission Board and to the fact that every Christian is a missionary.

Ten minutes later the copilot made his way back to David's seat and asked, "Are you really a missionary?"

"Yes. What is your name?"

"Claudio."

"I'm glad you have a Bible name."

The copilot wanted to see his name in the Bible. David showed it to him and then began to talk of the Bible truths relating to salvation. Before the plane reached Manaus, Claudio had made a profession of faith.

The following year, David was in Sao Paulo and asked the pastor of Pinherios Baptist Church about Claudio.

"He is to be baptized soon," the pastor said, "and so is his wife." (Usually in Brazil, new converts are not baptized right away, but first go through a period of study of the Bible and Baptist doctrines before they are baptized into church membership.)

*   *   *   *

David often spots something in surrounding circumstances which he can use to start a conversation naturally. Then he can move the conversation easily from the discussion of ordinary topics to spiritual ones.

Brazilian Baptists launched a Second National Campaign of Evangelism to be held in 1980 under the direction of Rubens Lopes. The first such campaign had been in 1965.

As chairperson of the Communications and Literature Committee for the 1980 campaign, David traveled often to Sao Paulo to meet with Lopes.

On one of these trips, he noticed that the young woman sitting by him on the plane was reading a magazine article, "Can Anybody Be Happy in This World?" He asked her opinion on the subject.

"Nobody is happy," she answered.

"I am happy. I have been married thirty-four years. I have a good wife, prettier today than when we first met." She laughed. He continued, "Six children, all happy."

He learned that the young woman was twenty-five, of a high class family. She said no one had ever before directly asked her about her religious beliefs.

On the plane, she made a decision to accept Jesus. At the airport, David introduced her to the pastor waiting for him so she would have contact with a church. David tries, when possible, to introduce a new convert to a pastor or church member so the convert will know where to go to find Christian fellowship and aid in the process of Christian growth.

On the next trip to Sao Paulo, David was at the Rio Airport waiting for the plane. An attractive young woman near him was complaining about the heat. He used the weather as a conversation opener and gave her a leaflet.

The young woman, an engineer, thirsty for more spiritual knowledge, started asking questions.

She said, "I have never had a Bible. Lately I have felt a desire to read one." He handed her a Bible and directed her to certain passages.

She asked, "How can a person be saved?" He explained to her the way and promised to send her a Bible correspondence course. He felt that the Holy Spirit had prepared her heart so she was not far from a decision.

*   *   *   *

On the way to Tokyo in 1970, where he was to be a speaker at the Baptist World Alliance Congress, David stopped in Taiwan to hold revival services in several cities. His English was not easy for

the Chinese interpreters to understand, for they had been accustomed to American English.

He stayed in the home of missionaries, Mary and Oz Quick in
Taichung. A young girl came every day to their home to help with
cooking and housework. Very shy, she didn't quite understand
when David would tease her. Though she had told the Quicks that
she was Catholic, they knew she never went to church.

David invited her to the services the first night, but she stayed
home. The next day he asked her why she didn't go. That night she
went but sat in the back seat. David had found out she was deaf
in one ear, so he asked why she sat in the back and told her he
wanted to see her in the front seat that night. To David, the servant
girl was a person important to God, not an evangelism project. He
has the faculty of identifying with rich and poor of every race. He
continued to witness to the girl during the day at home. That night
she went again and when David gave the invitation she went forward.

In the church that the Quicks attended was a family named
Chiang. The husband and wife and two girls were Christians, but
the two boys would not go to church.

The quicks took David to the Chiangs' gift shop. David and
Haydee were to celebrate their twenty-fifth wedding anniversary
that August. According to Brazilian custom, on the twenty-fifth
anniversary the couple has wedding rings made with a ring of silver
over half of each ring. Since the Chiang family made jewelry, David
wanted to ask the price of their rings.

One of the Chiang boys came into the shop. David knew from
conversation with the missionaries that this young man was not a
Christian. He began talking and joking with him. Finally, he asked
him what he was going to do that night. David was so persistent
there seemed no way the young man could refuse to attend the
service. He came to the services for two nights because David went
twice to his house to see him. The third night he made a profession
of faith.

While a guest at the China Hotel in Taipei, David began talking
to the hotel manager, James Chang. At first, it was hard for the two

to communicate. However, James eventually promised to go on Friday night to hear David preach at the Grace Baptist Church.

That night, Claude Rhea sang "Blessed Redeemer," and David spoke on the subject of all men being united in Christ. With the text Isaiah 53, he talked about men being scattered every one in his own way, until Jesus, the Redeemer, comes and changes that. Of the scores who made decisions Friday night, James was the first to walk forward.

David did not try to impose his beliefs on the young Chiang or on James Chang. He expected that if they went to the services God, through the Holy Spirit, would convict them of their sins and show them they needed the Savior. He had faith that God would prepare the hearts of his listeners.

After one of the meetings in Taipei, an old woman came up to David to ask why the people had come to the front during the invitation. She wanted to know why the people were crying.

Since she could not speak Mandarin, she had not understood the interpreter or the message. Now her granddaughter interpreted for her in Cantonese.

In simple words, vivid and colorful, minus long theological terms, David told her about Jesus' death for her. He gave a brief resumé of the sermon.

The woman said that she wanted to accept Jesus but did not understand how. David talked with her a long time and then left her with a counselor.

But the woman followed him downstairs and wanted to know more. He tried again to explain, but still she could make no decision. He went outside to wait for a taxi. Behold, he looked, and she was still following him!

"Now, now I am ready!" she cried. "I will accept Jesus as my Savior right now!"

*   *   *   *

During an evangelism campaign in Portugal in 1967, Baptists of Lisbon invited press representatives to a luncheon. Most of the reporters were afraid to go to the reception due to the extreme pressure of the Roman Catholic hierarchy and the censorship of all papers by the government at that time. They feared the wrath of both hierarchy and government censors. However, four or five reporters did attend.

One reporter who professed to be an atheist sat beside David during the luncheon and became intensely interested in the witness that he bore and his explanation of who Baptists are and what Baptists believe. David knew the Scriptures so thoroughly he could be fluent in giving reasons for his faith.

In fact, the reporter became so interested that a Sunday or two later he visited a Baptist church. The pastor was baptizing some of the new believers.

The newspaper man took a picture of a person being baptized, and that picture was printed on the front page of his newspaper the next day in a three-column photo over the caption, "Baptized as Was Jesus."

Half of an inside page was given to an explanation of New Testament baptism as understood, believed, and practiced by the Baptists. Joseph Underwood, Foreign Mission Board, SBC, was in Portugal for the campaign. He said this good publicity was largely the result of the extreme radiance, joy, and magnetic personality of David Gomes as he talked with that newspaper reporter.

*　　*　　*　　*

During the Crusade of the Americas in 1969, David preached in revivals in North Carolina. On the way, he boarded a Southern Airways plane in Miami.

After the plane had been airborne for a short while, the flight attendant walked to David's seat and asked, "Did you call me, sir?"

"No, I did not call you!"

Some time passed, and she returned and repeated the question.

"No, I have not called you, but it might be that God wants me to speak to you about him."

The flight attendant admitted that she had not been living a life that would glorify Christ. She made a decision that day in the plane to return to an active life in her church.

*　　*　　*　　*

In January, 1981, the Brazilian Baptist Convention met in Belem. David planned to go on January 20 but postponed his trip for one day in order to stay at the Mount Moriah camp because of a glorious meeting that was going on there. He arrived in Belem at 1:45 AM and could not find vacancy in any hotel. Returning to the airport in a taxi, he planned to await daylight there. However, he saw a house with a sign, "Room for Rent," and stopped to inquire. The man who lived there was named Joao Batista (John the Baptist), but he had never heard about God's love or of Jesus' death and resurrection. In the pre-dawn hours, David told him about Jesus. Joao Batista was saved.

The next morning David went to the Baptist seminary in Belem to seek temporary lodging and found the national pastors' conference in its final session. He told them of Joao Batista's acceptance of Jesus and set before them a challenge to pray and to witness. The ministers elected him their first vice-president, to be in office during the celebration of the centennial of Baptist work in the Country, 1982. Then the national convention elected Joan Soren president, to preside over the centennial commemorations.

In Rio, David was riding a public bus when the theme of religion came up. One man said, "I have been with spiritism, fetishism, and lots of others, and I have discovered that everything is vacant."

David waited. Before he left the bus, he whispered in the man's ear, "Jesus Christ is the way, the truth, and the life. Try him."

To David, the communication of his faith is so much a part of his life that it simply flows out of him without his realizing it. It is as automatic and natural to him as breathing. When he has light for those who are troubled and in the dark, he would not dream of keeping it to himself.

Haydee said, "Never does he lose an opportunity to tell a person about Christ. So many times he has done this at the banks where he keeps the Bible school money that I think those people will have no excuse to God when they are called home. All he wants is to make God known to people."

*   *   *   *

The Transforming Power of Christ

(From an address by David Gomes to the Fifth Baptist World Youth Conference, Toronto, Canada, 1958)

The Godhead was transformed—or God transformed himself. This was the transformation. . . . Jesus became a little baby. . . . He had to depend on his mother. He became flesh. This, my friends, is the greatest miracle that the world has ever seen—the miracle of God becoming man, of God becoming a child, of God leaving heaven and everything in heaven to come and dwell among us sinners.

The God that was transformed came to transform men. . . .

Last January we had our national convention in Brazil in the city of Salvador. Almost every pastor and missionary in Brazil attended that convention, but the main person in the convention was a man called Narciso Lemos. Narciso Lemos can hardly talk. He has never been to school, can barely read and write, but you know what happened to Narciso Lemos?

He was in one of the biggest gangster groups that existed in Brazil a few years ago. On one occasion he killed fifteen people and he has killed so many all together that he doesn't know how many. Narciso was arrested thirty times in Santos the year of his conversion. And then one day Narciso was walking down the street and met an old friend of his, one he knew from the time he was in that gang.

The friend said to him, "Well, Narciso, I'm glad to see you."

And Narciso replied, "I'm glad to see you too, Pereira." Narciso continued: "I'm glad that you came at this time because I am planning a little something to do in a few days and I want you to help me."

Pereira looked at him and said, "What are you going to do, Narciso?"

He said, "I am in need of money, and I am working out a plan to get money somewhere."

Pereira said, "You knew the old Pereira, but you don't know the new Pereira."

Narciso replied, "Why, you have white hair and you say you're new-born. You're not new-born. You're going crazy."

"No, I am new-born. I have been born again. You know the old Pereira, the one who used to go with you, but you don't know the new Pereira, the Pereira that has been transformed. The Pereira that Jesus has transformed you don't know. . . ."

Then Narciso said, "Well, let's go to the bar and get a drink. Then we'll discuss this."

Pereira said, "I don't drink any more. I don't drink anything alcoholic. I have been born again. I have been saved." Narciso mocked him saying, "That's why I don't care to be a believer. When you are a believer, you cannot drink and you cannot do what I like to do."

This was the beginning of the story of Narciso's being touched. He started reading the Bible and was converted a few months later. Jesus transformed him. He was saved and today he is a living witness for Jesus in the land of Brazil. And this is why when we went to the national convention in Salvador, the press wanted to know about Narciso Lemos, not the pastors and the missionaries who were on the program. Why? Because he was transformed by the great power of the God that was transformed. . . .

The transformed God can transform men. He can transform young people. . . . We've got to have Jesus as our Saviour and then we've got to have Jesus as our Lord, the Lord of all of us Brazilians and North Americans and Canadians and Africans and French and British. . . .

In all parts of the world we need missionaries. In some of the places in North America and maybe here in Canada there are thousands of young people who could be used but are not being used, who could preach and are not preaching, who could serve but are not serving. . . . These young people could serve the Lord day and night, from morning till night, but have not surrendered to Jesus as Lord of their lives, the Lord of their thoughts, the Lord of their walking, the Lord of their hearts, the Lord of their desires, the Lord of their money. Some use their money for worldly pleasures; others lose opportunities that are presented them, saying, "What am I here for? I don't have a thing to do." . . .

Last week I went downtown in Rio to pay my insurance. The

office was in a big building. I looked for a door, but saw no entrance. Finally I asked a man, "Will you please help me? How can I enter the building?"

He said, "If you want to go up, you've got to go down."

"Well, how can I go down?"

"Go around until you see a big entrance where you go down and as you go down you will find the elevator that will take you up."

If you want to serve the Lord, you must think seriously. If you want to go up, you have to come down first. Jesus is Lord because he came down a lot. He emptied himself so that we might be full. He denied himself so that he could give us the life we now have.

I like that verse in Hebrews that says that "Jesus died with a glad heart." It's in Hebrews, the 12th chapter, the second verse. "Looking unto Jesus, the author and finisher of our faith, who for the joy that was set before him endured the cross, despising the shame."

Did you ever realize that Jesus was crucified with a joyful heart? . . . Jesus had a smile when they were killing him. Do you know why? For the joy that was set before him. He was dying on the cross, but He had a smile on His face because He thought about me. He thought about you as the ones who would accept Him.

The One who will take you as you go down and keep you so that He can take you up and make you a glory to His name, a blessing to the world and happiness to many lives is Jesus our Lord.

23

A Fruitful Bough

Joseph is a fruitful bough, even a fruitful bough by a well; whose branches run over the wall (Gen. 49:22).

"For me, David Gomes is a living testimony of what God can do through a man who submits himself without reservation to God," wrote Delphino Eugenio Vieira, a Baptist pastor at Nicolopolis, Brazil, and president of the Bible School Board.

True, David has developed and used all the gifts God gave him for communicating the gospel. He keeps thinking of more creative ways to use his writing ability, his speaking ability, his music ability, his talent for relating to people, and his talent for teaching.

> Let the Saviour's gentle call
> Reach the heart of one and all,
> That the whole round world may know
> Christ is King, and Christ alone.

"Get a journalist. No pastor can do the job." C. E. Bryant protested from his Baptist World Alliance office in Washington, D.C.

"You have not met David," Missionary Edgar Hallock wrote back from Brazil. "Hold your fire until you see him at work."

It was 1959, and the tenth Baptist World Congress was going to be in Rio the following year. Hallock, in charge of local arrangements and Southern Baptist missionary, had written Bryant that David Gomes, a minister, had been put in charge of publicity.

Bryant's protest was without foundation. He made it because he knew something about the publicity difficulties Baptists faced in holding the world congress in Rio, the heart city of a nominally Roman Catholic country. Traditionally, non-Catholic groups had paid for any advertising space they got in Rio papers. And radio or television time had been out of the question.

Arnold Ohrn and C. E. Bryant landed at Rio airport about ten days before the congress opened. News photographers, reporters, television camera crews met their plane, as did Hallock.

"How much will all this publicity cost?" Bryant asked the missionary.

"Nothing. It's all free."

"But you told me last year we would have to pay for everything! What happened?"

Hallock answered in one word, "David."

Gomes welcomed Bryant with a warm embrace. The two of them worked closely for the next ten days. Bryant learned that when David had been appointed publicity chairman he had called each of the Rio papers and asked for an appointment with an editor. One had asked him, "Why don't you come down here about 3 AM?" doubtless hoping to discourage him. David was there next morning as the clock struck three, and the Baptists were in the papers.

On Saturday, before the congress opened, David took Bryant to a paper that had not, until then, run any Baptist news. "This editor has always refused to see me, but he will see us today," David said.

"How do you know?"

"I prayed about it," was the confident answer.

The two caught the elevator to the fifth floor. As the door opened, they were face-to-face with the chief editor. David reached both hands out to the man's shoulders and held him there. David spoke in a torrent of Portuguese for five minutes or more while the editor said nothing, and Bryant said nothing.

Then the editor turned to the American and spoke in English, "I attended a Protestant church up in Recife when I was a boy. My mother was a Presbyterian. We used to sing a song that went like this . . ." He hummed the melody.

David started singing, and the man joined him. Every editor in the big newspaper office gazed in amazement as these two sang the children's hymn, "Come to the Saviour." The Baptist World Congress was on page one of that paper Sunday morning.

David drove Bryant and Ohrn to a Rio television station one night, where they shared billing on the eleven o'clock news with a pretty brunette who had been chosen that day as Miss Brazil.

Next morning David visited Bryant and Ohrn in their hotel and ate breakfast with them, bringing his son and three of his daughters. He also brought a scrapbook full of material that had already been published advertising the congress.

"Tell me how you managed," Bryant begged. But David shrugged his shoulders at the attempt to praise him individually. "The Lord is good," was his reply.

The congress opened on a Sunday afternoon at 3 PM. Television crews moved in before noon and set up for a live broadcast of the opening.

Bryant walked into the Portuguese press room (David directed that one and Bryant the English language one) about 1 PM. David was sitting in a corner, sobbing his heart out, his head buried in his arms.

"What's the matter?"

"Oh, the Lord is so good! The Lord is so good!"

"Yes, I know, but why are you crying?"

"The television people!" David sobbed still louder.

"They are here. They have been setting up since eleven."

Then David told the story. He had begged a major network to telecast the Sunday opening, but they were planning to telecast a soccer game at Belo Horizonte. He had argued that the congress was more important. They said the sports broadcast had a paid sponsor. He had left the station disappointed on Friday afternoon but had not given up.

"I prayed and prayed that they would change their minds," he said. "And the Lord has made it rain in Belo. Oh, he is so good!"

> Flash the word that God is near
> O'er the air till all may hear.

On August 5, 1976, the national Radio and Television Board opened a new headquarters building in Campinas. Since David was vice-president of this Board, he presided at the opening ceremony.

Pastor Silas Melo from Bethel Church in Sao Paulo handed David a letter:

PASTOR DAVID GOMES:
   At this day when we have the great joy of inaugurating the new studio for Radio and Television of our national convention, I feel deep in my

heart gratitude for your life. You were the man to believe first in mass communications, and for 27 years you have been preaching the message on radio. Let me pay tribute to you.

Two years before, while David was prayer chairman for the Billy Graham Crusade in Rio in 1974, he had used radio and television extensively to ask for one thousand evangelical churches to be in prayer all night September 27, preceding the crusade.

> Print the Word till all may read:
> "Jesus is the friend in need."

Besides articles for denominational magazines and newspapers, he has written several books which have been popular in the evangelical book stores.

Questions the Bible Answers and *Bible Questions and Answers* are collections of questions he has discussed on his radio programs. *A Jew Called Abraham,* lessons from Abraham's life, was published in 1974. All profits from his books he has given toward expenses of the Bible School of the Air.

He translated *Rosa's Quest* which he offers to radio listeners who ask for it. Also he translated some of the works of D. L. Moody and W. T. Conner.

David's literary ability led to his membership in the Academy of Evangelical Letters (*Academia Evangelica de Letras*) of Brazil. This academy, patterned on one in Greece, has forty-eight patrons of forty-eight chairs. No new member is accepted unless the holder of a chair dies. All members of the nondenominational academy are evangelical Christians, and each has had at least one book published.

The purpose of the academy is to discuss and publicize the best books by Christian authors, who may or may not be members of the academy. Also the academy honors Christians who have contributed to the arts, studies the language, and concerns itself with improving members' writing.

David's entrance into the select group came at the death of his friend, Tancredo Costa, a Presbyterian minister, author, and professor of philosophy. Many Tuesday mornings, when the two drank coffee together, Cosa would say, "I hope one day to see you a member of the academy." Ironically, it was his own death that made that possible.

After Costa's death, while preaching in Belo Horizonte, the Justice Committee of the academy examined books and other published materials of each applicant. David tied with another man to be selected for the vacant chair. On a second ballot, he won.

David's installation ceremony took place June 5, 1976, at the Church of Hope, though ordinarily these ceremonies were held at the regular meeting place of the academy or in a public building.

Messages were read from the governor of the state and the mayor of the city, as well as from a representative of the national government in Brasilia.

David's twenty-five-page speech, titled "The Omnipotence of the Word," considered the Logos of God sent to the world. Later the speech was read to the state assembly and was recorded in the minutes of the assembly.

David has since served two terms as president of the academy.

Considering the value of the printed word in spreading the gospel message, David did not overlook the value of distributing Bibles and Scripture portions. Yet he had never given any thought to being president of the Bible Society until he had been elected to that office.

The Brazilian Bible Society publishes and distributes Bibles, New Testaments, and Scripture portions. Also the Bible Press furnishes Bibles, not only for Baptists but for all other evangelical groups in Brazil. (During World War II, Bible societies were unable to secure shipment of Portuguese Bibles into Brazil; therefore, the Bible Press of Brazil was organized in 1943, operated by the Baptist Publishing House.)

While David was in Jamaica in 1972, attending a meeting of the Executive Committee of the Baptist World Alliance, the Brazilian Bible Society elected him president. They had not previously consulted him, and he did not know until he heard the news in Jamaica that they were meeting. His acceptance of the position went back to the time in high school when he was elected Training Union president and determined always to take any responsibility offered him if he understood it to be God's orders.

The preceding year the Bible Society had awarded him the title of "greatest *divulgador* [or teacher] of the Bible" because of his radio Bible teaching. In addition, he had been a seminary professor for many years. He taught evangelism at the South Brazil Baptist Seminary but, in 1957, gave that up because of his constant Home Mission Board travels. Then in 1961, he began teaching theology and journalism on Monday nights and Tuesday mornings at Bethel Seminary. The request had come from Dr. Miranda Pinto, the founder, who was near death. This is a "faith seminary" which teaches according to Baptist beliefs but does not receive financial help from the Cooperative Program.

Also in 1973, David had been elected first vice-president of the national Baptist convention. In August, 1974, he was burning the candle at both ends. Besides his radio and church work, he was chairman of the Prayer Committee for the Billy Graham Crusade and in the midst of his four-year term as president of the Bible Society.

David would eat lunch at the office of the Bible Society about 1:00, stay there for two or three hours then return to the church to study and pray.

When the government began a literacy program, the Bible Society printed 700 thousand Scripture portions for children and grown-ups who were learning to read. These all were distributed and another edition printed.

Then came a crisis; money ran short. Fifteen employees were dismissed due to lack of money for salaries. The Bible building was mortgaged to a bank to provide capital for the work to proceed. To cut expenses, the headquarters was moved to Brasilia. Because of the distance, David declined to accept the presidency a second time but was elected honorary president for life.

In 1976, his last year as active president, the Society printed 291,736 Bibles, 103,211 New Testaments, and 18,949,271 Scripture portions. The 1972 figures had been 144,556 Bibles, 95,426 Testaments, and 7,166,773 Scripture portions.

Far and near the good news bring:
"Jesus Christ is Lord and King!"

David has not neglected his musical gift but often leads singing, translates hymns from English or Spanish into Portuguese, writes the words and occasionally composes the music, for hymns and choruses. In one instance, he wrote Christmas words to a German tune.

While preaching in a crusade in Argentina, he translated the revival theme song, "It Pays to Serve Jesus." Then, after a second visit to Argentina to be in a crusade with the missionary, Jack Glaze, he translated another hymn for Spanish.

Flying home from Buenos Aires, he kept humming "Sower of Peace," so he set up his portable typewriter and translated the hymn on the plane.

Sophia Regina met him at the airport; while the two of them were standing in line somebody stole his typewriter.

Shortly afterward, he attended a congress in Carolina. He and Pastor Nelson Nunes de Lima sang "Sower of Peace" together. Their duet was recorded with other selections on the record, *"A Sos Com Cristo."*

> Preach the Word on ev'ry shore
> Till all men do God adore.

Bill Agee, pastor of First Baptist Church, Hearne, Texas, Jim Lafferty, Rockdale, Texas, and David were eating lunch at Colombo's, a stately Rio restaurant. On occasion David would sneak a quick bite or two of seafood as if he would welcome the end of eating. Once he said between bites, "You know I'd rather preach any time than to eat." He meant that.

He is so full of vitality and life that his zest for living and serving God is contagious. All through the years since his ordination, he has frequently preached in revivals in churches and in area evangelistic crusades, almost always with an unusually good response from his listeners. He has preached in other countries including Australia, Argentina, Portugal, and Mozambique. When David went to Africa in 1974, the Baptist Convention of Mozambique had 400 members in 6 churches. While he preached at Lourenzo Marques, 250 conversions were counted.

The Baptist Ministers' Alliance of the state of Rio gave him a diploma during the Baptist Convention at Nova Friburgo in July, 1978. They officially named him "Father in the Faith."

In 1979, Falcao Sobrinho, general executive secretary for the Brazilian Baptist Convention, gave his evangelism class at the seminary an assignment. Each student was to plan a revival and tell whom he would invite to be the preacher. Sobrinho later told David that more than half of the group said they would invite David Gomes.

Because of his popularity as a preacher, David has been asked, "Why don't you go into full-time evangelism and hold wide-scale crusades like Billy Graham?"

He replies, "I am myself, and I must use my own style of evangelizing as the Holy Spirit directs me and in the way I feel the Brazilian people will respond to."

In 1963, while he was still with the Home Mission Board, David preached for a revival in the interior city of Divino. During a service that started at noon, attended by 150, he said to the congregation: "There were 3,000 decisions at Pentecost because there were 3,000 non-Christians present. If we want to win souls we have to get out and look for them." He suggested that they visit that afternoon and invite people to the night service.

At the end of his message, he held up two tracts and offered them to anyone who would promise to bring two visitors that night. Volunteers responded immediately.

On this trip to Divino, he had traveled almost all the way in a good bus on a paved road. He was reminded of traveling that same road twenty-three years before, the summer after he graduated from high school.

That first time he had gone part way by train, part way by bus over a rough road, and the last eighty kilometers on horseback. The town of Divino had gained electricity at sometime in the intervening years. A hotel had been built with five rooms. It was not luxurious, but the manager gave David a royal welcome.

The members worked hard visiting during the afternoon. That night the auditorium was filled. Many stood outside looking in. When David gave the invitation, eight raised their hands, saying they could accept Jesus as their Savior.

After the service three barefoot men came to greet him. They said they had walked fifteen miles from their homes.

"We want to thank you for bringing us the gospel twenty-three years ago. We still hoe in the fields for our living. We have no material comforts. We are without money. But the happiness and joy of being Christians is the same as then and continually growing."

David returned to the hotel with tears in his eyes. The trip twenty-three years before had been hard, but it had been worth all the hardships. Three people won to the Lord could have no price tag.

In revivals, as in his pastorates, David has always been ready to experiment with new techniques of trying to reach people for Christ. But he quickly points out that "this thing of innovative methods is so much of the Holy Spirit that I really deserve no honor at all. I try to depend upon the Holy Spirit completely."

While preaching at Penha, Sao Paulo, for three days, he began a study of Ezekiel, a young person in captivity who had visions of God. David said, "If we compare ourselves with each other, we might be able to boast, but never can we look at God (Isa. 6) and be able to boast." In this meeting at Penha, he suggested an all-night prayer meeting, from 11 PM until 6 AM. Two hundred stayed the whole time. During the night, David spoke four times.

Yearning over the crowds at Copacabana and a way to witness there, he and the executive committee of the Board planned a three-night preaching series for August, 1979. No suitable meeting place could be found, so it was held in open air. He reported, "Organization was poor, but the Lord worked; 125 accepted Jesus."

At a Youth congress in 1977, David spoke to university students. During the last session, sixty-two students came forward for various decisions and remained to pray for more than an hour. David wrote of this in his notebook, "Tears abounded. Confessions of sins were in great number. Later one of the students came to me in tears: 'Brother Gomes, I want your forgiveness. I came to criticize you. I did not want to hear you and yet God used you to reveal my sins. I will not kneel and ask your forgiveness, for I know you would not accept that, but in my heart I am kneeling.' "

During the summer of 1979, invitations came constantly from all over Brazil. In Vitoria da Conquista, he reported later, "the Holy Spirit took charge again. It was very cold, and people were not prepared for the cold wave. It rained the first night. The auditorium capacity was 300, but 134 found salvation. The mayor of the city was present. He said he had never seen a meeting like it in his life. He asked for a Bible correspondence course. I left that city to visit a farm. There I was able to witness to the farm workers, and six of them accepted Jesus. The last night I was in that area I spoke in the church at Itapetinga, and 55 made professions of faith, one a girl who had tried to commit suicide the day before."

In the state of Espirito Santo, David delivered a sermon on the Christian family. He gave an invitation in three stages. First, he asked for those who wanted to reconsecrate their homes and lives to God to come forward; several hundred crowded toward the platform. Others responded to the invitation to accept Christ or to return to church fellowship. Then in the third stage, he asked young people who were planning to be married soon and who felt the need of having God direct them in their family life to come forward. Many more came. Then he asked couples, engaged or married, to kneel in prayer together.

A week or two later he spoke in Maceio at a Youth congress where eight states were represented. Again he preached on the Christian family, each of the four times he was on program. The last day of the congress, beach time had been allotted at the close of the service. David spoke for ninety minutes and said, "I'm going to quit now. I have already robbed you of part of your beach time."

The young people answered as one, "Go on. We want to hear more Bible." He preached on until dinner time. David does not preach on families what he has not practiced. His own children reflect their parents' attitudes toward Christianity.

Ana Maria attended the seminary to become a teacher; married Reginalho Coutinho, a chemistry professor; and is the mother of a daughter.

Priscila married Israel Faria, a pastor, in 1971. Only six years later her husband died of cancer at age twenty-nine, leaving her with their children, Ana Raquel and Paulo. This has been one of the deepest sorrows of David's life and of his family. Priscila, a talented pianist, who studied at a conservatory of music, teaches piano at the Baptist Training School in Rio.

Esther Ruth married Geremias Bento da Silva on David's birthday, December 23, 1978. Geremias is associate pastor at the Church of Hope and assists at the camp. She directs choirs at the church and is a student at the Baptist Training School (1980). Their first son, Jonathan, was born in early 1981.

Marcos David was graduated from the university and is a civil engineer. His wife, Deisee, a postgraduate student in medical school, is pianist for the Church of Hope. They have a daughter.

Sophia Regina, after graduation from Gardner-Webb College in North Carolina, married Eduardo Steibel of Porto Alegre, September 17, 1977. They studied at New Orleans Baptist Theological Seminary and then transferred to Southwestern Baptist Theological Seminary in Fort Worth, where both received degrees in 1980. They returned to Rio where he is in charge of the administrative aspects of the Bible School of the Air, and she is producing the children's programs for radio and is teaching religious education at the Baptist Training School.

At seventeen, Elizabeth took an examination against stiff competition and won entrance directly to the university medical school, without having to do special preparatory study. As a boy, David had wanted to be a doctor; now he feels that his youngest daughter is fulfilling his dream.

24

A Tangle of Red Tape

Now unto him that is able to do exceeding abundantly above all that we ask or think, according to the power that worketh in us, unto him be glory in the church by Christ Jesus throughout all ages, world without end (Eph. 3:20,21).

If by faith
Enoch was taken up
That he should not see death, . . .

If by faith
Noah was warned by God
Of events yet unseen, . . .

If by faith
Abraham went out,
Not knowing where he was to go, . . .

If by faith
Sarah conceived in her old age,
Believing in God's promise, . . .

If by faith
The same Abraham offered up his son
And received him back, . . .

If by faith
Jacob, when dying,
Blessed the sons of Joseph, . . .

If by faith
Rahab, the harlot,
Gave friendly welcome to the spies, . . .

If by faith
Moses was hidden,
To be found, and to endure, . . .

If by faith
Gideon, Barak, Samson, Jephthah,
David and Samuel, were examples, . . .

If by faith
They crossed the Red Sea,
They saw the walls of Jericho fall,

They conquered kingdoms,
Enforced justice,
Received promises,
Stopped the mouths of lions,
Quenched raging fire,
Escaped the edge of the sword,
Won strength out of weakness,
Became mighty in war, . . .

Then you, O man of prayer,
How shall you not achieve
The Temple you would build;
For he who asks of the Father shall receive
By faith, that faith that makes for hope.

—Franklin Silva Filho
Translated by Joan Sutton
Dedicated to Pastor David Gomes

David went to Parana to speak at the First Baptist Church of Curitiba. The minister at breakfast time said to him, "You are thinking of putting up a building in Rio? How do you plan to finance it?"

"To tell the truth, I don't know. I am depending on God to tell me what to do and how to do it."

"Then why don't you call it the 'Building of Faith?' "

This seemed to be the ideal name, for David recalled one night at a church in Sao Paulo, where he had conducted a night of faith. He had spoken about Abraham and had knelt at the pulpit to show how Abraham bowed in faith before God.

After the Church of Hope had paid the bank for the corner lot, notification came that the land was mortgaged to INPS, a security department of the Brazilian government. The title was not a proper one. The church had nothing but a receipt, or an *alvara*, a certificate given by the government when the money was deposited.

When the company that sold the land actually went bankrupt, the church mobilized all efforts to obtain a second *alvara* which would place their situation in a new light. Nevertheless, a second *alvara* did no good. One of Brazil's best real estate lawyers told David, "You must give up hope for a deed and try to get your money back or else you will lose both land and money." The lawyer typed a petition, asking for the church's money back and stating that they would give up the land in return for the cash.

David took the petition but had no intention of signing it. He told the lawyer, "The Lord never walks backward. I don't believe he will just give us up." Yet everything seemed bleak.

On September 29, 1972, five lawyers met with the church council to discuss whether to try to get the money back. Three of the lawyers said to ask for the money back. One said the Lord would give the land. The other was undecided. David told them, "I want to thank God because I am positively sure he will give us the title." He named a committee to begin working out a thanksgiving service.

At the time of this meeting, David had cataracts on both eyes and could barely see. An opthalmologist had told him the cataracts were not ready for surgery.

During a convention in Rio in November 1972, a pastor friend grasped David's arm and demanded, "Don't you speak to me any more? Don't you love me any more?" David apologized, as he had to dozens of others.

"I have an uncle who is an opthalmologist," the friend said. "Let's go to see him." Next morning the doctor suggested that he operate on November 30. The church held a watch night of prayer on November 29.

December 1, the day after the surgery, David's eyes were still bandaged. The church's lawyer felt led of God to check on the court process for the deed.

At the court, he was told that the process was up for protest, at request of INPS, and that the Baptist group would have to pay an enormous fine, plus the debts of the bankrupt company.

The church lawyer searched until he found the lawyer to whom the process had been sent. Immediately the two recognized each other, for they had previously worked on a case together. The other man, not a Christian, asked the Baptist lawyer, "How do you keep looking so young?"

"I'm a Christian now, and I have come to represent the Church of Hope and the Bible School of the Air. I don't think you can blame them for the bankrupt company's debts! They have deposited three hundred thousand cruzeiros for the land and are ready to pay any balance due."

"All right, then. I will do all in my power to see that the court grants them the deed."

For three months, David had gone every day to INPS to find out how much more the church would have to pay and could not find out. Then while he was in the hospital blindfolded, the victory came. Thus he felt that God was saying to him, "I want you to know I am the Lord. I am doing this, not you."

On December 24, David's sight was restored. Though his eyes were not completely healed, he could go out; so the transaction for the deed was completed.

A date, May 5, 1973, was set for the thanksgiving service to thank God for: (1) the twenty-fourth anniversary of the Bible School of the Air, (2) the signing of the deed, and (3) the successful operation on David's eyes.

Four months later twelve thousand gathered in the Maracanazinho Stadium on a rainy afternoon. Television cameras captured the drama of the twenty-four thousand hands lifted in praise. Bill Ichter, Southern Baptist missionary, directed the two hundred-voice choir in singing "I Lift My Hands unto the Lord" to the accompaniment of an orchestra. A flash-card presentation was given by fifty girls from the Baptist Training School. David preached on "I Believe in Miracles."

Radio stations, newspaper, and television stations gave extensive coverage to the service. *Diaro de Noticias* printed the story on the first page of its Sunday edition. The governor and vice-governor of the state attended.

Before a building could be started, though, a large fee was due the government to prove the deed was legitimate. The church fought to prove it did not owe the fee. For the corner lot, they were fined about a thousand cruzeiros, and got the title. For the other lot they won the case and did not have to pay anything.

All of these procedures took time. Haydee worried about the load David carried and urged him not to make more debts. "You will kill yourself with so much burden about these things."

At last the contract for erection of the Building of Faith was signed on May 5, 1975, with the Presidente Company. The company agreed to construct a twenty-three-story building that would have a church auditorium, a chapel opening onto the street, studios for the Bible School of the Air, and other space to be used by the construction company.

It was too soon for anyone to breathe a sigh of relief. When the blueprints were presented to the government, another imposition came—a requirement for parking space inside the building. This would take up at least 40 percent of the space so would not be a satisfactory arrangement.

On April 5, 1976, the day that marked the sixth year of fighting to get the building started, the blueprints were approved with only two stipulations by the fire department.

In its tenth year, the Church of Hope had three hundred members and four missions. The members had hoped to lay the cornerstone for the Building of Faith on the church's tenth anniversary, August 14, 1976. This was not to be.

Members thought the government should not tell them how to build and should not require the inside parking space, so again they appealed to the courts. In the first and second instances they won; but the decisive turn would be the last. If the church lost in the third try, the government would nullify the appeal.

Finally the day came when the judge called the church representatives before the court. Three judges were to voice their opinions. About an hour before the trial was to begin, Haydee and David and other members of the church were seated in the courtroom.

Suddenly David felt he ought to go outside to pray alone. In a large men's lounge in the building, he decided to read his New Testament. As he opened the Book, his eye fell on John 11:11: "Lazarus sleepeth; but I go, that I may awake him out of sleep." Lazarus was dead, but he would be brought to life. David concluded that this meant they would lose in the court but would not lose the building.

When he returned to the courtroom, he whispered to Haydee, "I think we will lose, and yet I am sure we are going to win."

Lawyers for the church and for the state presented their facts. A young woman, Dr. Sonia, lawyer for the state, did an especially good job. Two of the three judges said they would vote in favor of the state.

Haydee said to David, "You don't look sad. You seem happy."

"Yes, I knew we would have to lose, so we could win the building."

The third judge did not cast his vote, as he wanted first to re-read the process. This would give the church the right to appeal to the Supreme Court in Brasilia. However, David told his lawyer, "I don't want to appeal anymore."

A day or so later, a former governor of the state told him, "I am glad you lost the appeal because if you had won, the government could have appropriated the two lots—made you the guardian or something like that—but you would never have been able to build there."

Oeanira, a nurse and a member of the Church of Hope, told her pastor: My mother is a servant in the home of Dr. Sonia, the defense lawyer for the state. My mother has been telling Dr. Sonia about our church and our plans for the Building of Faith. Dr. Sonia was concerned about what was best for the church. She told my mother that she did her best to make us lose because she knew that if we won, the government could take over both lots.

In amazement, David told his church members, "God has used his little child, a servant in the home of the lawyer, to further his cause!"

Still the new law in Rio, that no one could build in the inner city without adequate space for parking, remained in effect. The Presidente Company did not have such space.

A man who had some garages for sale told David, "You know a garage in the center of Rio is like a hen that lays golden eggs. Never would a person sell a treasure like that! But I will sell to you for two hundred thousand dollars [Brazilian currency] one space for a car." Of course, his offer was refused.

On December 28, 1976, a special dinner and business meeting was held at the church. One member said he thought it was time to give up the idea of a Building of Faith. "It seems to me we should build a small building where the church could meet, with some extra space for the radio studio. We should give up having a building of such magnificence."

Though most in the crowd did not pay attention to what the man was saying, he spoke the feelings of a particular group who thought that the building would never be erected. David knew that a good many were growing skeptical.

One day David's secretary, a seminary student, said, "Pastor, I came across a construction site where a parking garage has been started, but the building has been stopped for some reason. It is near the church."

The building belonged to a company that had gone bankrupt and had to quit building the parking garage. David found the man, De Paoli, who was head of the company.

De Paoli could not do anything because of his bankruptcy, but he put David in touch with another company. This second company could not build either, but they put him in touch with a third company—Carlos Magalhaes Company.

Carlos Magalhaes Company signed a contract to construct the Building of Faith. Carlos had married a Baptist, who was a member of First Baptist Church in Rio. He told David that when they first started to receive funds for the building, his wife had given some money.

The church was supposed to pay a fine of $7,500 to quit the contract with the Presidente Company which had no garages or parking space. Carlos Magalhaes called the other company and offered to negotiate for the blueprints.

Carlos Magalhaes said, "We will build twenty-two floors of the Building of Faith. We will give the Bible School of the Air the second, third, fourth, fifth, sixth, and twenty-second floors, and we will have the other sixteen. We will build in return for use of the valuable land."

For the size of the building they were told they would need 107 vacancies for parking. Carlos Magalhaes had exactly 107 spaces for parking.

These plans were completed in 1977. David's son, Marcos, had graduated from the university in the spring. As an architect, he gave David some advice about the best finish for the exterior of the building.

A model of the planned building was made, and the church had picture postcards made of the model.

On November 15, 1977, another thanksgiving service was held at the Maracanazinho Stadium. This time the people praised God that the building was on its way to a beginning. At the service, the father of Carlos Magalhaes—Alcides Magalhaes—was converted and made a public profession of faith. (Soon afterward he fell ill of cancer.)

It poured rain all day on November 15, a small deluge. Though over five thousand people came, the planners had hoped for many more. The rain may have been an omen of the disaster that was about to strike.

25

The Building of Faith

They that trust in the Lord shall be as Mount Zion, which cannot be removed, but abideth forever (Ps. 125:1).

On the day after the thanksgiving service, the Magalhaes Company began preparations to build. One week later, the work stopped. The government had sent a statement that 176 parking spaces would be required instead of the 107 originally quoted.

The construction company agreed to pay for the additional spaces. A few weeks later, on January 24, 1978, while David was in Recife, the company followed through on its agreement. However, as David wrote in his notebook, "The devil had the need to put in another difficulty." The Bible school's request for additional time to obtain the extra spaces had been denied. The whole process concerning the building permit had been sent to the archives. This could mean that all the efforts to have a building had gone down the drain.

When David heard this information January 26 from the lips of a woman, a clerk in the construction company office, he told her, *"Os que confiam no Senhor sao como os montos de Diao que nao se abalam, mas permanecem para sempre"* (Ps. 125:1). Right then he called the office staff together, in the company's building, to pray with him, asking the Lord's help in removing this new obstacle.

David remembered that a Brazilian pastor, Xavier Assumpcao, had once told him, "The name David seems to me a prophecy because you've been before Goliath, have suffered much, and yet have overcome."

After the prayer, the clerk said to him, "I don't remember the number of the law under which this project was prepared. If it came before the law 322, it can be restored."

David answered, "It will be restored, for there is a hymn that says, 'Faith is never defeated,' and the number of that hymn is 322."

Since on March 1 David meant to go to Brazilia, the Magalhaes representatives asked him to try to get an order from the president of the country to approve the project. However, a Christian judge in Brazilia advised that such a step might hinder rather than help.

While inside one of the bowl-shaped Congress buildings in Brasilia, David by chance met a well-known congressman who knew about the planned Building of Faith and asked about its progress. As a result, the following Monday this congressman traveled to Rio. Through his efforts, the process for the building permit was brought back for approval.

On April 27, a new contract was signed. At last, David held in his hand the license to start the building. The congregation was asked to move to another place of worship so the old building could be torn down.

About two hundred yards away from the church stood an old building for rent. Generally landlords in the area charged from two thousand to five thousand dollars rent a month. At first, the owner of the old building said he would charge the church twenty-five hundred dollars a month but later agreed if they did not use the ground floor, but only the second and third stories, he would charge six hundred dollars a month.

The Church of Hope, in the midst of painting the rented place and moving into it, considered plans for a cornerstone laying ceremony.

Sunday afternoon, August 27, hundreds of Christians covered the grounds where the Building of Faith was to be constructed.

In the first part of the program, "Praise, Only Praise," choral groups from Higienopolis Baptist Church sang. Professor Tabitha Miranda led a prayer of dedication. The congregation sang "Break Thou the Bread of Life" and a special hymn written by a young seminary student called "Edifice of Faith."

In the second part of the program, surprise guests arrived: Jimmy Allen of San Antonio, Texas, president of the Southern Baptist Convention, USA, and Raymond Kolb, the SBC Foreign Mission Board's field representative for Brazil.

Allen spoke enthusiastically to the crowd, interpreted by David:

Pastor David Gomes and friends of this church: I bring you greetings from your thirteen million brothers and sisters in Christ who are a part of the Southern Baptist Convention of the USA. We join in rejoicing along with all Brazilan Baptists with this marvelous time of the laying of the cornerstone for your building. I believe that your church is well named because you have great hope. The name of David Gomes across our whole Baptist world is known for the kind of faith that he has exercised in his leadership. I'm delighted with the fact that this moment is a time of great triumph for you.

When the children of Israel came to the time to cross the river Jordan, in the book of Joshua, God told them to pick up stones from the bottom of the river Jordan which was now dried up. As they placed the stones out in a monument beside the crossing of the river, the Bible says they did that so that their children could ask, What mean these stones? They could then say, These stones mean that we are claiming the promise of God. God has promised the land, and now we possess it. These stones mean that we have seen the barriers fall that kept us from claiming the promises. The river Jordan stopped us, but the Lord stopped the river.

As your children's children look at this building and say what do these stones mean, you will be able to say: These stones mean that we are claiming the promises of God. These stones mean that God has removed every barrier before us. These stones mean that there is greater victory in the future than we have known in the past.

God will use this church, along with all the fellowship of Brazilian Baptists, to reach more than a million people by 1981.

One hundred years of Baptist witness in Brazil will be the celebration of new victories to come. You are part of this, you are at the heart of it and God will bless you in it.

Your Baptist brethren all over the world will rejoice that God has given you the victory because you have had the faith. Pray for Southern Baptists that we will have the same kind of faith that you have had here in this place.

Soloist Paul Moreira thrilled everyone with his beautiful voice. The atmosphere was alive with enthusiasm, deep joy, and heartfelt praise.

Some of the representatives who came from the different national and state boards to bring greetings were: Lester Bell (National Executive Board), Victor Davis (Religious Education and Publications Board), Sophia Nichols (WMU of Brazil), Glen Grober (Evangelism Board), Antonio Lopes (Foreign Mission Board of Brazil), Ubiracy Gusmao (Building and Loan Board), Joaze Paula (State Executive Board), Rev. Quintanilha (Brazilian Bible Society), Jim and Maxie Kirke (missionaries), and hundreds of others from dozens of churches, besides the members from Esperanca (Hope) Church.

Not being able to attend personally, the governor of the state sent Victor Alves de Brito to represent the state of Rio de Janeiro.

Brazil's outstanding Baptist singer, Feliciano Amaral, delighted the audience with a hymn that expressed the deep feeling of gratitude that filled everyone's heart. Also, state representative, Daniel Silva, equally blessed with a beautiful voice, sang a hymn.

Although many people had to leave before the ceremony was over due to church obligations, others arrived late, thus making a total of nearly a thousand people who participated in some part of the cornerstone ceremony.

A choral group from the First Baptist Church of Rio presented a musical number entitled "Cornerstone," written especially for this occasion by Celso de Oliveira.

As is the custom, an urn to be placed in the hole dug for the cornerstone was opened in order that those who so desired could place something that would be of historical value. Newspapers of the day, publications of the Bible School of the Air, copy of the Holy Bible, poems, emblems, church bulletins from the churches represented, and coins of the present currency were deposited in the urn before it was lowered into the ground.

A copy of the Bible was presented to each of the four owners of the construction companies who would build the Building of Faith. One of the four men declared, "This is the first Bible I have ever received as a gift."

Music was presented by the Youth choir of the Church of Hope. Closing words by Delphino Vieira, the president of the Bible School of the Air Consulting Council, reminded the people that just as Jacob's experience at Peniel was a born-again experience for him, this ceremony was a decisive moment in the journey that lies ahead for the Bible School of the Air.

Within a few months, the church members heard the news that they would have to move again. The owner of the rented building had gotten an unexpected opportunity to sell the building and land. If he broke the lease, technically he would owe the church at least three hundred thousand cruzeiros.

Instead of angrily demanding payment, David handled the matter in a tactful way, talking kindly to the man and praying with him about what should be done. Since the owner knew he was in a tight spot, he promised to pay the church's light bill for three months, give the church six months free of rent, plus two hundred thousand cruzeiros and moving expenses.

In April, while driving pilings for the foundation, a construction crew observed that if they continued, the whole building next door would collapse at any time. They stopped work.

In July, when David returned from a ten-day trip to Bahia, he and a group of church members met with Carlos Magalhaes, who reported, "Friends, it seems the prayer of your pastor was strong. The Andolfo Lindenberg Company is in trouble. If our builders had started the walls, we would have needed to wait over two years to continue, but since they had not begun the walls, there is no problem for us. We have signed with another company to continue in the place of Lindenberg's." The builder projected a completion date of October, 1982, exactly one hundred years after the first Portuguese-speaking Baptist church was organized in Brazil.

September 1, an investigator of the incident decided to take another measurement of the lot before giving his final opinion. He discovered the lot was twenty-two meters wider than the deed showed it to be. A wonderful surprise! The building could be enlarged. Another small miracle. David told Haydee, "Only God could have stopped the builders, and arranged this remeasurement."

Again, as many times before, David saw the truth of Ecclesiastes 7:8: "Better is the end of a thing than the beginning."

"What Is That to Me?"

Frank Moran of Morehead City, North Carolina, flew to Rio in 1968 to attend the Pan-American Congress of Baptist Men. While in Brazil he heard of the Church of Hope and went there to worship at a noonday service.

When Haydee saw Frank and several other North Americans enter the sanctuary, she joined her husband at the pulpit to interpret his message in English.

During a conversation later, Frank asked David how he could help him most in the task of spreading the good news. He expected the answer to be a request for prayer and financial aid, and hoped that would be the reply, for then he could say in his heart, "These things I have done since my youth."

But David's answer startled him, "Brethren, give yourselves completely to the Lord. Be as missionary in North Carolina as you would desire me to be missionary in Brazil."